LARRY SANG'S

CHINESE ASTROLOGY & FENG SHUI GUIDE

2020

The Year of The Rat

鼠

with Lorraine Wilcox

LARRY SANG'S

The Year of The Rat

ASTROLOGY AND FENG SHUI GUIDE

Original Title:
**Master Larry Sang's 2020 The Year of the Rat
Astrology and Feng Shui Guide**

Published by: The American Feng Shui Institute
7220 N. Rosemead Blvd., Suite 204
San Gabriel, CA 91775
Email: fsinfo@amfengshui.com
www.amfengshui.com

Written by:
Master Larry Sang

Edited by:
Lorraine Wilcox

Cover Design, Illustration & Layout by:
Heidy Hon

Acknowledgment

This book would not be possible without the assistance of our brightest students and dear friends. Thank you Lorraine Wilcox for your wise input, editing, and translation. Thank you Heidy Hon for coordinating the layout, book cover, illustrations and keeping everything together, Chris Shaul for your expertise support and Zihan Zhang (張子涵) for your assistance with Sifu's calligraphy. Most of all, thank you to my wife Salina for your tireless love and support.

-Larry Sang

Please Read This Information

This book provides information regarding the subject matter covered. The authors are not engaged in rendering legal, medical or other professional advice. If you need medical or legal advice, a competent professional should be contacted. Chinese Astrology and Feng Shui are not get-rich-quick or cure-all schemes. Changes in your life will happen as fast as you are ready for them. Be patient in your study of Chinese Astrology and Feng Shui.

The authors have tried to make this book as complete and accurate as possible. However, there may be typographical or content mistakes. Use this book as a general guide in your study of Chinese Astrology and Feng Shui.

This book was written to educate and entertain. The authors, distributors and the American Feng Shui Institute shall have neither liability nor responsibility to any person with respect to any loss or damage caused, or alleged to be caused by this book.

The following pages of predictions will help you understand trends as they develop through the coming year. Please keep in mind that they are somewhat general because other stellar influences are operative, according to the month, date and exact minute of your birth. Unfortunately, we cannot deal with each person individually in this book.

Table of Contents

How to find Your Animal Sign

In order to find your correct animal sign, as well as understand why the Chinese calendar begins in February, and not January, it is important to have a little understanding of the two different Chinese calendars. As with most things Chinese, we look at the Yin and Yang. In Chinese timekeeping, there is a Yin Calendar (Lunar calendar) and a Yang Calendar (Solar calendar).

The Lunar Calendar

The Lunar calendar is perhaps the best known and most popular of the two. Chinese Lunar New Year is frequently celebrated with a lot of pageantry. It is used in one type of Chinese Astrology called Zi Wei Dou Shu, and also in Yi Jing calculations.

The Solar Calendar

The Solar calendar is less well known. The early Chinese meteorologists attempts to gain insight into the cycles of the seasons. From this study, this developed the Solar calendar. This calendar is used in the form of Chinese Astrology called Four Pillars, as well as in Feng Shui. The Chinese were very accurate in their studies. Without computers, and using only observations, they mapped a solar year of 365 days. They missed the actual timing of a year by only 14 minutes and 12 seconds.

The solar year is divided into 24 solar terms. Each lasts about fifteen days. Spring Begins (lichun) is the name of the first day of Spring, and the first solar term. It is exactly midway between the winder solstice and the spring equinox. This is why it always falls on February 4th or 5th. We begin the five elements with Wood, so the Chinese New Year begins with a Wood month, whether in the Lunar or the Solar calendar. These concepts are derived from the Yi Jing.

人是自己幸福的设计者

Man is the artificier
of his own happiness

How to find your Animal Sign

To find your animal sign, Start with your birth date. If it is before February 4th (Spring Begins), use the prior year for the Chinese calendar. If it is after February 4th, then use the same birth year. If it is on February 4th, then you need the time of the birth to accurately determine the birth animal. This information is contained in the Chinese Ten-Thousand Year Calendar. (The American Feng Shui Institute has one available as an ebook at www.amfengshui.com). In the following pages, the birth years are listed for each animal, but remember, if your birthday is before February 4th, use the previous year to determine the animal.

The Twelve Animals

Rat 鼠	Ox 牛	Tiger 虎	Rabbit 兔
1924, 1936, 1948, 1960, 1972, 1984, 1996, 2008, 2020	1925, 1937, 1949, 1961, 1973, 1985, 1997, 2009, 2021	1926, 1938, 1950, 1962, 1974, 1986, 1998, 2010, 2022	1927, 1939, 1951, 1963, 1975, 1987, 1999, 2011, 2023
Dragon 龍	Snake 蛇	Horse 馬	Sheep 羊
1928, 1940, 1952, 1964, 1976, 1988, 2000, 2012, 2024	1929, 1941, 1953, 1965, 1977, 1989, 2001, 2013, 2025	1930, 1942, 1954, 1966, 1978, 1990, 2002, 2014, 2026	1931, 1943, 1955, 1967, 1979, 1991, 2003, 2015, 2027
Monkey 猴	Rooster 雞	Dog 狗	Pig 豬
1932, 1944, 1956, 1968, 1980, 1992, 2004, 2016, 2028	1933, 1945, 1957, 1969, 1981, 1993, 2005, 2017, 2029	1934, 1946, 1958, 1970, 1982, 1994, 2006, 2018, 2030	1935, 1947, 1959, 1971, 1983, 1995, 2007, 2019, 2031

FORTUNES OF THE 12 ANIMALS

The Rat

1936, 1948, 1960, 1972, 1984, 1996, 2008, 2020

Note: The New Year begins February 4ᵗʰ

Good fortune awaits the Rat in the Rat year of Gen Zi 庚子. The Tai Sui 太歲 Star strengthens two auspicious Stars, the Jiang Xing 將星 Star and Golden Cabinet 金匱Star making this a positive year. Career and money prospects are to your satisfaction. This is an excellent time to push ahead with personal plans. The best luck is in the spring and winter months. Trying something new or a career change can bring about positive results. However, being safe is still the best policy. Do not be too ambitious, to avoid ending up with nothing. There are signs of financial mishaps in long distance travel during the beginning to middle of summer. Be careful of overspending. Health-wise, there are no serious problems, but the common health complaints are allergies and insomnia. Watch out for injuries by sharp metallic objects because of the Sword Blade 劍鋒Star enters your Ming palace. Where romance is concerned, lovers and spouses tend to be temperamental, so frequent squabbles will take place. It will be a year of hits and misses for the single Rat. Those who you have no feelings for will be after you, while your intimate partner or the one you love may walk away. For those who are married, you and your spouse will have different opinions that cause stress or heated discussion.

鼠

Your Benefactor is: Dragon

(1928, 1940, 1952, 1964, 1976, 1988, 2000, 2012)

12 Month Outlook For The Rat

Solar Month	Comments
1st Month Feb 4rd - Mar 4th	A rewarding month. Most things are to your satisfaction.
2nd Month Mar 5th - Apr 3rd	There are signs of unexpected gains and a benefactor coming forward.
3rd Month Apr 4th - May 4th	You may be in a low mood. Beneficial time for venturing overseas.
4th Month May 5th - Jun 4th	Strong Peach Blossoms. Be cautious of gossip.
5th Month Jun 5th - Jul 5th	You can easily feel depressed and moody.
6th Month Jul 6th - Aug 6th	Take care of your physical health.
7th Month Aug 7th - Sep 6th	Be cautious of money loss.
8th Month Sep 7th - Oct 7th	Average luck. Things may suddenly turn sour.
9th Month Oct 8th - Nov 6th	Money luck is strong. Things come out well.
10th Month Nov 7th - Dec 6th	A very auspicious time to offer or receive a marriage proposal!
11th Month Dec 7th - Jan 4th	This is a good time to plan or to learn something new.
12th Month Jan 5th - Feb 3rd	Don't expect too much. Be tolerant. Your are prone to get angry over some trivial matters.

The Ox

Note: The New Year begins February 4ᵗʰ

It will be a year of bountiful gains for the Ox. Opportunities will come knocking at your door but stiff competition lies ahead. In comparison with 2019, the male Ox has improved luck, as a result of the Tai Yang 太陽 Star shinning above. It brings good money-making opportunities for the self-employed. With an auspicious Sui He 歲合 Star, it is a good time to expand your social circle to give your career an extra boost. This is a good year to begin your goals that will lay a firm foundation for the future. Investment plans are best carried out in early spring. With the Yin Sha 陰煞 Star in Ming Palace, the female Ox does not share the same auspicious luck as the male Ox. However, luck has improved a lot from last year. Females will encounter backstabbers easily. You can not afford to be careless when dealing with female colleagues or friends. It is best to think before you speak. While there are no signs of major health problems, it is advisable to get plenty of rest. Hui Qi 晦氣 Star, explains the physical discomfort caused by your moodiness. Where affairs of the heart are concerned, singles will meet their ideal life partners. Females born in 1985 or married couples should avoid getting involved in a love triangles.

牛

Your Benefactor is: Dog
(1934, 1946, 1958, 1970, 1982, 1994, 2006, 2018)

12 Month Outlook For The Ox

Solar Month	Comments
1st Month Feb 4rd - Mar 4th	Luck is steady and smooth.
2nd Month Mar 5th - Apr 3rd	This is a relatively favorable month for travel, but exercise caution and heed your hunches.
3rd Month Apr 4th - May 4th	Strong Peach Blossoms. This is a joyous time for females. There are complicated relationships for males.
4th Month May 5th - Jun 4th	An extra good month for artists and writers! A good time to learn something new.
5th Month Jun 5th - Jul 5th	Luck and mood is like a bouncing ball – Up and Down.
6th Month Jul 6th - Aug 6th	Be on guard. You are likely to incur unnecessary expenditures.
7th Month Aug 7th - Sep 6th	Money luck is "easy come easy go".
8th Month Sep 7th - Oct 7th	Money luck is strong. Big gains, small losses. The harder you work the more you gain.
9th Month Oct 8th - Nov 6th	The Celebration Star is shining inside the door. You will feel happy and enjoy life. Be careful to avoid cuts and travel accidents.
10th Month Nov 7th - Dec 6th	Avoid visiting the sick and attending funerals.
11th Month Dec 7th - Jan 4th	Average luck. Pay attention to your health to avoid minor illness.
12th Month Jan 5th - Feb 3rd	Auspicious luck. You can get what you hope for.

The Tiger

1926, 1938, 1950, 1962, 1974, 1986, 1998, 2010

Note: The New Year begins February 4ᵗʰ

On the surface, it seems like a good year for the Tiger. The truth is, it is fraught with hidden dangers. Salaried workers will have better luck than the self-employed. Employers will be bogged down by endless problems like manpower shortage. Risky investments and business deals are not to be taken for face value. Money luck is like a bouncing ball: up and down. This is not a year to be speculative. Salaried workers will gain recognition for their performances. With Yi Ma 驛馬 Star in the Ming Palace, a change of working environment or moving is highly possible. But be forwarned against betrayal by someone you trust. In late autumn be wary of vile characters around you. Try to do everything yourself and be humble at all time. Money prospects are average to good. The harder you work the more you gain. Health-wise, do not neglect minor illnesses and be careful of injury to any of the four limbs. The presence of Xong Men 喪門 Star in the Ming Palace, is a warning to take care of the elderly in your family. Where romance is concerned, due to the Gu Chen 孤神 Star entering your door, do not expect too much from relationships. Frequent bouts of loneliness and depression may lead to severe mental distress. Take good care of yourself. Married couples should refrain from quarreling. Tolerance is the keyword.

Your Benefactor is: Sheep
(1931, 1943, 1955, 1967, 1979, 1991, 2003, 2015)

12 Month Outlook For The Tiger

Solar Month	Comments
1st Month Feb 4rd - Mar 4th	Busy month. A change of working environment is highly possible.
2nd Month Mar 5th - Apr 3rd	Strong Peach Blossoms energy around you. Every thing is joyous!
3rd Month Apr 4th - May 4th	One can easily feel depression and moody.
4th Month May 5th - Jun 4th	Be conservative. Be alert for signs of overspending.
5th Month Jun 5th - Jul 5th	Be careful of being cheated. Keep on high alert. A wrong decision may result in financial losses.
6th Month Jul 6th - Aug 6th	Career and money prospects are good.
7th Month Aug 7th - Sep 6th	Money luck is strong. An auspicious time for you to plan something new or switch jobs.
8th Month Sep 7th - Oct 7th	Good time to develop something new. Salaried workers can expect a promotion.
9th Month Oct 8th - Nov 6th	Stay flexible throughout the month. Carefully look for the jade among the rubbish.
10th Month Nov 7th - Dec 6th	Watch out for unstable health. An unexpected occurrence could affect your health
11th Month Dec 7th - Jan 4th	Money luck is strong. You may receive some unexpected benefits.
12th Month Jan 5th - Feb 3rd	This is a lucky month with peace and harmony.

The Rabbit

1927, 1939, 1951, 1963, 1975, 1987, 1999, 2011

Note: The New Year begins February 4th

With one of the Wealth Tai Yin 太陰 Star in the Ming Palace, the Rabbit will find the Rat year blessed. Your career will soar to great heights, bringing you wealth and fame. Investments will prove to be most rewarding. This is an excellent year for business and career. You can see big benefits and big profits as a result of your hard work. The busier you are, the more benefits you will receive. While money luck is good, the rewards will come from the effort you put into your work. Not as a result of a windfall. Gou Jiao 勾絞 Star and Guan Suo 貫索 Star in your door. It is advisable not to act as a guarantor to others in the spring. Apart from migraines and allergies caused by stress, there are no real health concerns. The presence of the benign Hong Luan 紅鸞 Star will put your close relationships in the spotlight. Those born in 1951 or 1975 may have to undergo surgery. Romance is like milk and honey! Rabbits will easily fall in love with Rats and Roosters, this is especially true in the Rat year. It is going to be a beautiful year for romance. For the married Rabbit, if there were misunderstandings and arguments in the past, you should take this time to improve the situation. The current luck will assist you to offer apologies that wyour partner.

兔

Your Benefactor is: Monkey
(1932, 1944, 1956, 1968, 1980, 1992, 2004, 2016)

12 Month Outlook For The Rabbit

Solar Month	Comments
1st Month Feb 4rd - Mar 4th	Auspicious luck! You will feel great. All your work will be highly rewarded.
2nd Month Mar 5th - Apr 3rd	Your thinking will be strongly influenced by others, especially a partner. Minor changes will occur.
3rd Month Apr 4th - May 4th	Stay flexible throughout the month. Carefully look for the jade among the rubbish.
4th Month May 5th - Jun 4th	Be conservative. Be alert for signs of overspending.
5th Month Jun 5th - Jul 5th	Good for venturing overseas.
6th Month Jul 6th - Aug 6th	Strong money luck. You may discover a new source of income.
7th Month Aug 7th - Sep 6th	Auspicious Stars Tian Xi and Fu Xing shine above! Good in all aspects.
8th Month Sep 7th - Oct 7th	Everything you do will be nearly effortless.
9th Month Oct 8th - Nov 6th	Slow down and double check all documents before you sign.
10th Month Nov 7th - Dec 6th	Conditions stimulate you to try something different.
11th Month Dec 7th - Jan 4th	This is a rather auspicious month. Career will be smooth sailing.
12th Month Jan 5th - Feb 3rd	Travel can put you in contact with a person who benefits your career in the future.

The Dragon

1928, 1940, 1952, 1964, 1976, 1988, 2000, 2012

Note: The New Year begins February 4th

With San Tai 三臺 Star and Hua Gai 華蓋 Star visits the Ming Palace. The Rat year is basically stable for the Dragon. Do not try to set your expectations too high or you will be spreading yourself too thin. Remember, too much self-esteem will lead to negative results. Be prepared for any contingency and you will go through the year without any mishaps. Extra care should be taken when dealing with anything in April and August. Keep alert and do not take risks if you are doubtful. Overall, things will be relative peaceful for you. Be wary of trouble from colleagues or subordinates. Those born in 1964 and 1976 in particular may find themselves being betrayed by coworkers. Where money luck is concerned, reasonable income from hard work can be expected. Health-wise, except for minor illnesses, the Dragon will generally be healthy. Avoid stress brought on by overworking. Plenty of rest is recommended. Take preventive measures against colds during winter. Where romance is concerned, the single Dragon will have no trouble finding aprospective spouse. Though, it is better to take the initiative. For married couples, disputes with your loved one will occur frequently. This is especially true with those born in 1952 and 1964. Try to be more understanding towards each other.

Your Benefactor is: Horse
(1930, 1942, 1954, 1966, 1978, 1990, 2002, 2014)

12 Month Outlook For The Dragon

Solar Month	Comments
1st Month Feb 4rd - Mar 4th	Days seem unusually long because of your moodiness.
2nd Month Mar 5th - Apr 3rd	Avoid visiting the sick and attending funerals.
3rd Month Apr 4th - May 4th	You are likely to incur unnecessary expenditures. Be on your guard, keep expenses under control.
4th Month May 5th - Jun 4th	Good for venturing overseas.
5th Month Jun 5th - Jul 5th	Auspicious Stars shine above! Work is highly rewarded.
6th Month Jul 6th - Aug 6th	Luck is smooth for everything you plan. Salaried workers can expect a promotion.
7th Month Aug 7th - Sep 6th	You may have to take care of something you thought was already settled.
8th Month Sep 7th - Oct 7th	Do not rush in affairs. Luck is mixed between good and bad.
9th Month Oct 8th - Nov 6th	Auspicious luck is returning. You will see much hope and many opportunities.
10th Month Nov 7th - Dec 6th	Good in all aspects. You are busy and marching forward smoothly.
11th Month Dec 7th - Jan 4th	A physically busy month.
12th Month Jan 5th - Feb 3rd	Luck is good. This is a great time to expand or start a new project.

The Snake

1929, 1941, 1953, 1965, 1977, 1989, 2001, 2013

Note: The New Year begins February 4th

 An auspicious Yue De 月德 Star in the Ming Palace. Tian Xi 天喜 Star, and Tian De 天德 Star are together in the Career Palace. Therefore, 2020, the year of the Rat heralds exceptionally good fotune for the Snake. It is a good year for self-employed to make new plans and investments. Excellent progress and bountiful gains can be expected. Good luck coupled with hard work will bring about substantial profits. Money may come from unexpected sources. Expand your social circle to give your career an extra boost. The only warning is to avoid being too arrogant and greedy. Otherwise, you can get yourself in trouble. A promotion and pay rise will come the way of the salaried worker in autumn or winter. This is a year for you to demonstrate your abilities. Be humble and cooperate with others. Success will belong to you. Health-wise, eventhough there are no signs of major health problems, it is advisable for you to get plenty of rest. Stress and insomnia are two problems you should watch out for. Where romance is concerned, for those of you already in love, you are in a harmonious relationship. If you are looking for love, unforgettable romance will come your way. In summertime you could easily fall in love. Married couples should be wary of the intrusion of a third party.

Your Benefactor is: Tiger
(1926, 1938, 1950, 1962, 1974, 1986, 1998, 2010)

12 Month Outlook For The Snake

Solar Month	Comments
1st Month Feb 4rd - Mar 4th	Stay flexible throughout the month. Carefully look for the jade among the trash.
2nd Month Mar 5th - Apr 3rd	Keep on high alert. Any wrong decisions may lead to financial losses.
3rd Month Apr 4th - May 4th	Be alert for signs of discomfort due to stress.
4th Month May 5th - Jun 4th	Be conservative. There are signs of conflict.
5th Month Jun 5th - Jul 5th	Watch out for the flu or cuts. Do not visit sick people.
6th Month Jul 6th - Aug 6th	Normal luck. Relaxation is the top priority.
7th Month Aug 7th - Sep 6th	Unstable luck. An unexpected event could affect your health or employment.
8th Month Sep 7th - Oct 7th	Luck is strong. Your money and career will be in good shape
9th Month Oct 8th - Nov 6th	Good opportunities. Be ready to take advantage of a change.
10th Month Nov 7th - Dec 6th	Busy month. You may frequently feel unwell or moody.
11th Month Dec 7th - Jan 4th	Strong Peach Blossoms. This is a joyous time for females. But not beneficial for males.
12th Month Jan 5th - Feb 3rd	A work project or a relationship -- may be less than harmonious.

The Horse

1930, 1942, 1954, 1966, 1978, 1990, 2002, 2014

Note: The New Year begins February 4ᵗʰ

This year the Po Sui 破歲 or Year Breaker 歲破 for the Horse. This is a challenging year. Being adaptable will help you ride over any crisis. Work will require all of your concentrated attention. It will guide you to be innovative in coping with challenges. Inauspicious Da Hoa 大耗 Star, and Disaster Sha 災煞 Star, make this year quite unstable. You may encounter difficulties one after another. Salaried workers or self-employed, it will take double effort to receive a single gain. The presence of the Da Hoa 大耗 indicates a strong sign of substantial loss of money, so stay away from financial speculation. In addition, the Horses should be wary of taking undue risks since this year is a time where changes take place faster than you can imagine. Inauspicious Tian Ku 天哭 Star and Lan Kan 闌干 Star indicate unhappy things or legal matters. This is a year to play defense. Do not trust anyone blindly lest you get cheated. Keep your emotions under tight control in all situations. Health-wise, there are no life-threatening illnesses. Common health complaints for the Horses are painful joints, rheumatism, and so forth. In matters of the heart, there is no sign of a permanent commitment. Married Horses may find themselves unnecessarily prolonging a relationship. A third party may put your marriage on the rocks.

Your Benefactor is: Rabbit

(1927, 1939, 1951, 1963, 1975, 1987, 1999, 2011)

12 Month Outlook For The Horse

Solar Month	Comments
1st Month Feb 4rd - Mar 4th	Be on guard. It is likely to incur unnecessary expenditures.
2nd Month Mar 5th - Apr 3rd	Do not trust anything blidly, otherwise you may find yourself in an embarrassing situation.
3rd Month Apr 4th - May 4th	Strong in money luck but be conservative. Signs of conflict.
4th Month May 5th - Jun 4th	A good time for learning something new.
5th Month Jun 5th - Jul 5th	Luck is mixed. Don't expect too much.
6th Month Jul 6th - Aug 6th	Take care of elderly family members. Be cautious with your own health as well.
7th Month Aug 7th - Sep 6th	Powerful sign of luck. Work hard you will achieve favorable results.
8th Month Sep 7th - Oct 7th	Luck and harmony are in sync. You will receive unexpected benefits by working with others.
9th Month Oct 8th - Nov 6th	This is a relatively favorable month for travel.
10th Month Nov 7th - Dec 6th	Auspicious luck! This is a rewarding month for both romance and business.
11th Month Dec 7th - Jan 4th	This month is filled with depression, confusion, and frustration. Take good care.
12th Month Jan 5th - Feb 3rd	Do not rush in affairs. Your mental processes are not as good as usual.

The Sheep

Note: The New Year begins February 4th

The Rat year brings good tidings to the Sheep. Zi Wei 紫微 and Long Te 龍德 auspicious Stars shines above giving you energy and enthusiasm. You will be busy, ambitious, assertive, and willing to fight for what you want. Your wit will come in handy. Career and money prospects are particularly rewarding for the self-employed. Although obstacles may stand in the way of your career, you will see sunshine after the rain. Grab the good opportunities as your career will take a big step forward. A promotion and pay raise will come for salaried workers. Make full use of the year to strive for what you want. However, due to the inauspicious Stars as Sudden Failure 暴敗 and Sui Sha 歲煞, you must be careful if you plan to make investments. Do not make risky investments. It is best to cut down your losses by avoiding gambling and financial speculation altogether. Health-wise, you may suffer from ailments of the digestive and circulatory systems. Love is very rosy this year and there is great opportunity for marriage for the Sheep. Female Sheep should be wary of flattering men, otherwise trouble will follow. If your are an unhappily married Sheep, this is a good year to recover and return to the honeymoon phase!

羊

Your Benefactor is: Snake
(1929, 1941, 1953, 1965, 1977, 1989, 2001, 2013)

12 Month Outlook For The Sheep

Solar Month	Comments
1st Month Feb 4rd - Mar 4th	You can easily feel depressed and moody.
2nd Month Mar 5th - Apr 3rd	This is a relatively favorable month for travel, but exercise caution and heed your hunches.
3rd Month Apr 4th - May 4th	High spirits give you ample energy and vitality.
4th Month May 5th - Jun 4th	Luck is mixed. A low-key approach works best.
5th Month Jun 5th - Jul 5th	Relaxation is the top priority. Put aside all thoughts of work responsibilities. Rest and enjoy the company of family members.
6th Month Jul 6th - Aug 6th	Opportunity lies ahead. You need to be well prepare and fight for it.
7th Month Aug 7th - Sep 6th	Business ventures overseas are promising.
8th Month Sep 7th - Oct 7th	This is a favorable month. Money and career aspects are to your satisfaction.
9th Month Oct 8th - Nov 6th	Auspicious Stars shine above! This is a good month to get married.
10th Month Nov 7th - Dec 6th	Strong Peach Blossoms. This is a joyous time for females but complicated relationships arise for males.
11th Month Dec 7th - Jan 4th	Money luck is "easy come, easy go".
12th Month Jan 5th - Feb 3rd	Do not bet on the outcome of a race or game if a good deal of money is involved.

The Monkey

Note: The New Year begins February 4th

The Rat year may not be an easy year for the Monkey. With White Tiger 白 虎 and Fei Lian 飛廉 in the Ming Palace, there will be danger in legal entanglements. Do not use underhanded ways to make money or you may get into legal problems. Because of the Backstabber 指背 star, you will encounter back stabbers and find it easy to arouse misunderstandings between your friends. Be humble and avoid being arrogant. But don't be depressed, the Brilliant Money Lu Cun 祿存 Star is in the Ming Palace, so money luck is generally strong! This Rat year will provide Monkeys with more opportunities. It is nearly certain that 2020 will bring Monkeys at least one dramatic change in their career. Whether this change is voluntary or not, you should take heart that these transitions hold a wealth of potential for you. There may be a slight change in your fiscal position, but nothing to fret about. Your health will generally be good. Avoid overworking and stay away from abusing alcohol or overindulging in sex. Peach Blossoms is strong. Romance is colorful. Make sure whoever you love will be loved fully and wholeheartedly. Be loyal to your loved one. Do not try to put your feet on two different boats or you will fall into the Water and be full of regret. Married couples will find it easy to have a third-party intruder.

Your Benefactor is: Ox
(1937, 1949, 1961, 1973, 1985, 1997, 2009, 2021)

12 Month Outlook For The Monkey

Solar Month	Comments
1st Month Feb 4rd - Mar 4th	Promote your interests this month, and it can be a time of accomplishment.
2nd Month Mar 5th - Apr 3rd	Money and career will go well.
3rd Month Apr 4th - May 4th	Travel is not advised this month. Matters at a distance are not beneficial. Luck goes hand in hand with your hard work.
4th Month May 5th - Jun 4th	Take care of your physical health. An old sickness could return.
5th Month Jun 5th - Jul 5th	Luck goes hand in hand with your hard work.
6th Month Jul 6th - Aug 6th	Creative and mental energy peak simultaneously. New opportunity is just around the corner.
7th Month Aug 7th - Sep 6th	Conditions are not static, someone closed may be making plans causing some turmoil and mixed feelings.
8th Month Sep 7th - Oct 7th	Bathe in the spring breeze! Everything is so enjoyable.
9th Month Oct 8th - Nov 6th	Confusing. Nothing is as clear as it seemed last month
10th Month Nov 7th - Dec 6th	This is a particularly good time to be starting a new job or learning something new.
11th Month Dec 7th - Jan 4th	Do not ignore talk of a possible lawsuit. Problems may arise.
12th Month Jan 5th - Feb 3rd	A busy month. Do not go too fast. Slow down and double check all documents before you sign.

The Rooster

1933, 1945, 1957, 1969, 1981, 1993, 2005, 2017

Note: The New Year begins February 4th

The new year will begin with a fortunate trine aspect linking Tian Xi 天喜, Tian De 天德 and Fu Xing 福星 stars. This is no better time to make a change than now. A dream can come true regarding a financial or sexual matter that involves your love life. Be prudent and realistic, then work hard to accomplish your goals.

Even when you encounter some obstacles, they can be overcome and ultimately benefit you. With extraordinary good fortune this year, progress can be made on a large project if you break it down into manageable parts that enable you to see results as you go along. Cooperation is the best method of attack. Alone you can get a lot done, but as part of a team there is nothing to hold you back. Be free with praise and congratulations. Health-wise, there are signs of bleeding. Avoid overworking and stay away from liquor and undesirable liaisons. Those born in 1945 and 2005 may have to undergo surgery. With Tao Hua 桃花 star and Xian Chi 咸池 star in the Ming Palace, chances romantic encounters are plentiful. A certain relationship may lead to marriage, so treat it seriously. However, stay alert for clues indicating scandals caused by Peach Blossoms, because of the Juan Se 卷舌 Star of gossip is mixed in with these two Peach Blossoms stars. Those who are married must stay away from extramarital affair. Otherwise, there are endless troubles.

Your Benefactor is: Rat

(1924, 1936, 1948, 1960, 1972, 1984, 1996, 2020)

12 Month Outlook For The Rooster

Solar Month	Comments
1st Month Feb 4rd - Mar 4th	Totally enjoyable! Happy and smooth like a spring breeze upon you.
2nd Month Mar 5th - Apr 3rd	Be conservative. Things are changing. Communications are apt to be misinterpreted or misunderstood.
3rd Month Apr 4th - May 4th	Average luck. A minor illness may show up.
4th Month May 5th - Jun 4th	Auspicious Stars shine above! Money and career are in good sight.
5th Month Jun 5th - Jul 5th	Good news can be expected within the family! Luck is smooth.
6th Month Jul 6th - Aug 6th	Beneficial to travel – the sun will shine on you. But if you stay at your birthplace, your luck is up and down.
7th Month Aug 7th - Sep 6th	Money luck and Peach Blossoms are strong. Happy feelings all the time!
8th Month Sep 7th - Oct 7th	A month of mixed good and bad. Avoid being arrogant.
9th Month Oct 8th - Nov 6th	Keep on high alert. A sign of relationship breakup or cuts.
10th Month Nov 7th - Dec 6th	Beware of being betrayed or sold out by others. Where money is concerned, do not trust or give loans.
11th Month Dec 7th - Jan 4th	Plot future plans with care; the benefits will be everything you could hope for.
12th Month Jan 5th - Feb 3rd	Auspicious money luck. For salaried workers, there is a future promotion or pay raise. Be alert of potential backstabbers.

The Dog

1934, 1946, 1958, 1970, 1982, 1994, 2006, 2018

Note: The New Year begins February 4th

With the Float and Sink 浮沉 Star inside the Ming Palace, the Dog's luck floats and sinks this year. Failures comes as easily as success. A project that seems promising may have to be shelved for later due to lack of interest or financial backing. The power of the Jia Shen 解神 Star and Tian Jia 天解 Star will make unhappy relationships and situations fade away. Therefore, do not throw away your hard work, later in the year you may be able to revive it. In dealing with people should be low-key and humble all the time. This is a beneficial year for Dogs to take a new study or learn something new; it will help advance your future career. Money luck is like a bouncing ball, up and down. Risky investments on the whim should be avoided. Keep expenses under control or else financial affairs will consume a lot of your time and energy. Health-wise, there are signs that the Dog over-works this year. Take preventive measures against chronic illness caused by stress. Romance will not be smooth sailing. 2020 will seem unusually long to female Dogs because of their moodiness caused by the influence of Gua Su 寡宿 Star. Do not take the relationship for granted even if you are in love, or a third party may come along and ruin it. Married couples will run hot and cold and quarrels will be easily aroused.

狗

Your Benefactor is: Pig
(1935, 1947, 1959, 1971, 1983, 1995, 2007, 2019)

12 Month Outlook For The Dog

Solar Month	Comments
1st Month Feb 4rd - Mar 4th	Average luck. You may fall sick easily for no apparent reason.
2nd Month Mar 5th - Apr 3rd	Be conservative. It will be easy to arouse gossip and fighting causing by misunderstanding.
3rd Month Apr 4th - May 4th	Luck is strong. Grab the opportunities to expand your business.
4th Month May 5th - Jun 4th	This month holds good fortune for proceeding with something new or expand your career.
5th Month Jun 5th - Jul 5th	A busy month. Though there is pressure on your job, money and career are in good view.
6th Month Jul 6th - Aug 6th	Good opportunities come your way. Money and career aspects are to your satisfaction.
7th Month Aug 7th - Sep 6th	Luck is average. You may frequently feel unwell or moody.
8th Month Sep 7th - Oct 7th	Lots of things are bothering you (gossip, etc.) Keep calm and say less. Beware of burglary.
9th Month Oct 8th - Nov 6th	Some obstacles lie ahead. Don't retain high expectations or be greedy about money matters beyond your capability.
10th Month Nov 7th - Dec 6th	Put off any uncertain projects until you are sure you have examined all the angles.
11th Month Dec 7th - Jan 4th	The celebration Star is shining inside the door. You will feel happy and enjoy life.
12th Month Jan 5th - Feb 3rd	Be cautious of everything. There is a sign of bleeding. Drive defensively.

The Pig

1935, 1947, 1959, 1971, 1983, 1995, 2007, 2019

Note: The New Year begins February 4th

The Pig's luck alternates between good and bad in the Rat year. Most of the time, things and people are not quite what they appear to be. Personal effort is required at a higher level than normal to accomplish your tasks. Co-workers are apt to be argumentative and ready to pick fights. Think before you speak, and speak before you act. Getting along with co-workers requires patience. A low-key approach is advised. Do not attempt to dodge responsibilities for an error of judgment or a misreading of facts may arise. During 2020, financial matters will attract your attention. You will have some expenses and you will wonder about ways to increase your income. Due to the Wang Shen亡神 Star in the Ming Palace, someone you have been counting on as a supporter is beginning to back off. Promises that were made are not reliable. Relying on your own efforts is the best approach. Promises should be accepted with a grain of salt. Relying on promises made by others can be harmful. With the presence of the Bing Fu 病符 Star, you may fall sick easily for no apparent reason. Those born in 1935 should refrain from visiting the sick or attending funerals. In romance, it is going to be a relatively quiet year. For those who are married, your spouse needs your care and understanding.

Your Benefactor is: Rooster
(1933, 1945, 1957, 1969, 1981, 1993, 2005, 2017)

12 Month Outlook For The Pig

Solar Month	Comments
1st Month Feb 4rd - Mar 4th	You'll better off physically if you get extra sleep. Your energy level will be low and your resistance weakened.
2nd Month Mar 5th - Apr 3rd	Money luck is smooth sailing and things are average to good.
3rd Month Apr 4th - May 4th	Auspicious Stars are shining above! Substantial gains can be expected.
4th Month May 5th - Jun 4th	Average luck. You feel busy physically and mentally.
5th Month Jun 5th - Jul 5th	Things are pleasant and enjoyable for the females but not for males.
6th Month Jul 6th - Aug 6th	Your mate or another relative can turn you from optimistic to gloomy with words or a hostile look.
7th Month Aug 7th - Sep 6th	Partly sunny skies. Luck will be bumpy. When you gain, watch out for a possible loss
8th Month Sep 7th - Oct 7th	There are signs of financial losses. Be alert for signs of overspending.
9th Month Oct 8th - Nov 6th	You will experience tense relationships with people. There are signs that family disharmony may occur.
10th Month Nov 7th - Dec 6th	Someone you rely on for support is being influenced in a new direction.
11th Month Dec 7th - Jan 4th	Keep on high alert. Avoid alcohol and staying out late. There are signs of health problems.
12th Month Jan 5th - Feb 3rd	Small things are apt to irritate you. Travel is not advisable.

信任少數人
不害任何人
愛　所有人

Trust only a few,
harm nobody,
and love all

LI MING

TABLE 1 立命 LI MING (establish fate): STEP 1: DETERMINE YOUR PALACE

立命 LI MING for 2020

This is another system for making annual predictions:

- First, use Table 1, based on your month and time of birth.
- Take the results of Table 1, and use them in Table 2, along with your year of birth, to find the palace of Li Ming for 2020
- Once you know the palace of Li Ming, read the prediction that follows for that palace.

Birth Hour:		Born After:											
		Jan 21 1st Month	Feb 19 2nd Month	Mar 20 3rd Month	Apr 20 4th Month	May 21 5th Month	Jun 21 6th Month	Jul 23 7th Month	Aug 23 8th Month	Sep 23 9th Month	Oct 23 10th Month	Nov 22 11th Month	Dec 22 12th Month
Zi	11pm-1am	Mao	Yin	Chou	Zi	Hai	Xu	You	Shen	Wei	Wu	Si	Chen
Chou	1-3am	Yin	Chou	Zi	Hai	Xu	You	Shen	Wei	Wu	Si	Chen	Mao
Yin	3-5am	Chou	Zi	Hai	Xu	You	Shen	Wei	Wu	Si	Chen	Mao	Yin
Mao	5-7am	Zi	Hai	Xu	You	Shen	Wei	Wu	Si	Chen	Mao	Yin	Chou
Chen	7-9am	Hai	Xu	You	Shen	Wei	Wu	Si	Chen	Mao	Yin	Chou	Zi
Si	9-11am	Xu	You	Shen	Wei	Wu	Si	Chen	Mao	Yin	Chou	Zi	Hai
Wu	11am-1pm	You	Shen	Wei	Wu	Si	Chen	Mao	Yin	Chou	Zi	Hai	Xu
Wei	1-3pm	Shen	Wei	Wu	Si	Chen	Mao	Yin	Chou	Zi	Hai	Xu	You
Shen	3-5pm	Wei	Wu	Si	Chen	Mao	Yin	Chou	Zi	Hai	Xu	You	Shen
You	5-7pm	Wu	Si	Chen	Mao	Yin	Chou	Zi	Hai	Xu	You	Shen	Wei
Xu	7-9pm	Si	Chen	Mao	Yin	Chou	Zi	Hai	Xu	You	Shen	Wei	Wu
Hai	9-11pm	Chen	Mao	Yin	Chou	Zi	Hai	Xu	You	Shen	Wei	Wu	Si

Notes:

These months are different from the solar (Feng Shui/Four Pillars) months, and also are different from the lunar months. They begin on the *Qi* of the *Twenty-Four Jieqi*. If born within a day of these month dates, please consult a *Ten-Thousand Year Calendar* to determine exactly which is your birth month in this system. It is not necessary for you to understand the Chinese terms in the tables. Just follow the tables to the correct palace for you.

TABLE 2 立命 LI MING (establish fate): STEP 2: PALACE FOR A ZI (RAT) YEAR

立命 LI MING for 2020

Li Ming:	Birth Year:											
	Rat Zi	Ox Chou	Tiger Yin	Rabbit Mao	Dragon Chen	Snake Si	Horse Wu	Sheep Wei	Monkey Shen	Rooster You	Dog Xu	Pig Hai
Zi	Shen	You	Xu	Hai	Zi	Chou	Yin	Mao	Chen	Si	Wu	Wei
Chou	You	Xu	Hai	Zi	Chou	Yin	Mao	Chen	Si	Wu	Wei	Shen
Yin	Xu	Hai	Zi	Chou	Yin	Mao	Chen	Si	Wu	Wei	Shen	You
Mao	Hai	Zi	Chou	Yin	Mao	Chen	Si	Wu	Wei	Shen	You	Xu
Chen	Zi	Chou	Yin	Mao	Chen	Si	Wu	Wei	Shen	You	Xu	Hai
Si	Chou	Yin	Mao	Chen	Si	Wu	Wei	Shen	You	Xu	Hai	Zi
Wu	Yin	Mao	Chen	Si	Wu	Wei	Shen	You	Xu	Hai	Zi	Chou
Wei	Mao	Chen	Si	Wu	Wei	Shen	You	Xu	Hai	Zi	Chou	Yin
Shen	Chen	Si	Wu	Wei	Shen	You	Xu	Hai	Zi	Chou	Yin	Mao
You	Si	Wu	Wei	Shen	You	Xu	Hai	Zi	Chou	Yin	Mao	Chen
Xu	Wu	Wei	Shen	You	Xu	Hai	Zi	Chou	Yin	Mao	Chen	Si
Hai	Wei	Shen	You	Xu	Hai	Zi	Chou	Yin	Mao	Chen	Si	Wu

Notes:

★ Take the Palace of Li Ming, found in Table 1, and compare it to the year of birth to find the palace for 2020 a Zi (Rat) year.

★ Use January 21st as the beginning of the new year for finding the birth year. If the date falls within one day of January 21st, check in a *Ten-Thousand Year Calendar* to be sure. If the birth date is between January 1st and January 20th, consider the person as belonging to the previous year in this system.

★ The predictions described below go from January 20th, 2020 until January 19th, 2021.

Zi

The Tai Sui Star combines with two auspicious Stars to make this a positive change prone year. A profitable investment opportunity awaits the self-employed. Salaried workers may receive a promotion or pay raise. Make full use of the year by working hard and fighting for what you want. Be careful of overspending. There are signs of financial mishaps in traveling long distance.

Chou

Li Ming is good in all four seasons. Tai Yang together with other auspicious Stars are shining above. Take advantage of this good luck to achieve your goals. Sources of money moves upwards. A benefactor of the opposite sex will show up for females, while a benefactor of the same sex will show up for males. Regarding job changes, early spring and late summer are the best time to do it.

Yin

Be patient and do not get discouraged easily. It is not a year to expand or to be overly optimistic. Whatever is accomplished requires double efforts to receive a single gain. Indulgence brings unexpected consumption of small things. Yi Ma Star shines above, there are good opportunities for money luck if you go far from your current working place. There are signs of job changes or house moves.

Mao

The four seasons pass by happily. With Hong Luan Star shines above, singles will easily find a suitable life partner. There are signs of marraige. Any relationship that is in the budding stage may move ahead if you are willing to be more aggressive. Females will enjoy better money luck and career will go smoothly compared to males. Be cautious of your speech. There are signs of conflict in relationship.

Chen

If Li Ming is here, This is an excellent time to embark on higher education or learn something new. Students can expect good academic results. 2020 will seem unusually long due to your moodiness. You could advance rapidly in your career or move up socially if you are willing to make an effort. Observe good eating habits and watch out for sprains and fractures.

LI MING PALACE READING

Si

Inauspicious Stars fall together in this palace. If Li Ming is here, it is a year to be conservative and not to be aggressive when embarking on a new career. Be forewarned of some obstacles you may encounter. There is a lot confusion in dealing with things. It is unfavorable for legal affairs. Investment should be made only after careful consideration

Wu

This year Sui Po is in Ming Palace, and Tai Sui is in opposite, It will be a year of breakthrough or change. Conflict with others will arise easily. Not a year to expand or be overly optimistic. Things beyond your control suddenly change. With an inauspicious Da Hao Star, it is a sign of increased unnecessary expenditures. Watch out for cash-flow problems and budget wisely. It is unfavorable for legal affairs.

Wei

Zi Wei and Long De auspicious Stars shines above, giving you energy and enthusiasm. You will be busy, ambitious, assertive, and willing to fight for what you want. Your wit will come in handy. While this is a relatively good year, caution and care must be taken to prevent acts of sabotage arising from jealous by others. The best policy is to be humble at all time to prevent nasty situations.

Shen

It is significant that Lu Cun Star falls in this palace. If Li Ming is here, you could make use of the strong money energies to help you reach a financial goal. There may be a slight change in your fiscal position due to the presence of an inauspicious Star Dai Sha, but nothing to fret about. Avoid overworking. You may get sick if you over-extend yourself.

You

The year will begin with a fortunate trine aspect linking Tien Xi, Tien Te and Fu Xing. Dreams can come true regarding financial or love matter. Be prudent and realistic, and work hard to accomplish your goals. It is going to be a beautiful year for romance. Those who are married should avoid getting involved in extramarital affairs.

LI MING PALACE READING

Xu

Inauspicious Stars gather together. It is appropriate to be cautious and prudent in all matters. This year is not a time to be speculative. Be careful of injuries to any of the four limbs by sharp Metallic objects. The presence of Tian Jie Star will assist in resolutions when unhappy matters arise. Take care of elderly family members. Avoid visiting hospitals or attending funerals.

Hai

If Li Ming here, do not trust anyone blindly lest you get cheated. You may suffer financial losses through fraud. Jointly held finances will require attention. This warning must be considered. Don't hold higher expectations about money beyond your ability to earn it. You may fall sick easily for no apparent reason..

LIU REN

LIU REN (六壬)(小六壬)

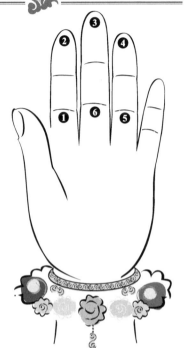

1. Great Peace
2. Back & Forth
3. Hastening Happiness
4. Red Mouth
5. Small Auspiciousness
6. Empty & Lost

Calculation:

When something out of the ordinary spontaneously happens,
you can determine the meaning of the omen with *Liu Ren*.
Here is the calculation:

1. Use the left hand. Start in position 1, Great Peace (大安 da an)
   and always move clockwise.
2. Count clockwise through the six positions for today's *lunar*
   month. The Great Peace position corresponds to the first lunar
   month. (Refer to *Ten-Thousand Year Calendar* page at the end
   of this *Guide*. Find today's date, then read the month number at
   the top of the column).
3. Count the position found in Step 2 as the first day of the lunar
   month. Count clockwise through the six positions to today,
   the current day of the lunar month. (Find today's date in the *Ten-
   Thousand Year Calendar* page, then read the day number on the
   side at the end of the row).

4. Count the position found in Step 3 as the first double hour. Count clockwise through the six positions to the current double hour.
5. Look up the interpretation of this palace on page 44 - 45.

Hour Table

Hour	During Standard Time	During Daylight Savings Time
1	11 pm - 1 am	midnight to 2 am
2	1 - 3 am	2 - 4 am
3	3 - 5 am	4 - 6 am
4	5 - 7 am	6 - 8 am
5	7 - 9 am	8 - 10 am
6	9 - 11 am	10 - noon
7	11 am - 1 pm	noon to 2 pm
8	1 - 3 pm	2 - 4 pm
9	3 - 5 pm	4 - 6 pm
10	5 - 7 pm	6 - 8 pm
11	7 - 9 pm	8 - 10 pm
12	9 - 11 pm	10 - midnight

Note: for 11 pm to midnight during standard time, use the next day's date. For example, if it is 11:15 pm on February 12th, then count it as February 13th.

Example: July 15h, 2015, 5:30 pm

A. Start in Position One.

B. July 15th is in the column that says 5th month at the top.
   So we go to Position Two.

C. July 15th is the 30th day of the 5th month.

D. Start where we left off in Position Five and call that 1.
   Count clockwise to the 30th position from there: Position Four.

E. Start in Position Four and count for the hour.

F. During Daylight Savings Time, 5:30 pm is the 10th hour. Count 10 positions, with Position Four and call that 1, and end up in Position Two.

This is the outcome:

Position Two is **Back and Forth**
Read the interpretation on the next page and apply it to the situation.

Interpretation

1. Great Peace (大安 da an):

The person in question has not moved at this time. This position belongs to Wood element and the East. Generally in planning matters, use 1, 5, and 7. This position belongs to the four limbs. Helpful people are found in the Southwest. Avoid the East. Children, women and the six domestic animals are frightened.

In Great Peace, every activity prospers. Seek wealth in the Southwest. Lost items are not far away. The house is secure and peaceful. The person you expect has not left yet. Illness is not serious. Military generals return home to the fields. Look for opportunities and push your luck.

2. Back and Forth (留連 liu lian):

The person you expect is not returning yet. This position belongs to Water element and the North. Generally in planning matters, use 2, 8, and 10. This position belongs to the kidneys and stomach. Helpful people are found in the South. Avoid the North. Children wander the road as disembodied spirits.

With Back and Forth, activities are difficult to achieve. You have not adequately planned for your goals. Official activities are delayed. Those who have gone do not return from their journey yet. Lost items appear in the South. Hurry and ask for what you want and you will get results. But guard against gossip and disputes. Family members for the moment are so-so.

3. Hastening Happiness (速喜 su xi):

The expected person arrives shortly. This position belongs to Fire element and the South. Generally in planning matters, use 3, 6, and 9. This position belongs to the heart and brain. Helpful people are found in the Southwest. Avoid the South. Children, women, and animals are frightened.

With Hastening Happiness, happiness arrives. Seek wealth toward the South. Lost items are found between 11 am and 5 pm if you ask a passerby about it. Official activities have blessing and virtue. Sick people have no misfortune. Auspicious for the fields, house, and the six livestock. You receive news from someone far away.

4. Red Mouth (赤口 chi kou)

An inauspicious time for official activities. This position belongs to Metal element and the West. Generally in planning matters, use 4, 7, and 10. This position belongs to the lungs and stomach. Helpful people are found in the East. Avoid the West. Children are bewildered young spirits.

Red Mouth governs quarrels and disputes. Be cautious about legal matters. Quickly go search for lost items. Travelers experience a fright. The six domestic animals give you trouble. The sick should go to the West. Furthermore, you must guard against being cursed. Fear catching epidemic diseases.

5. Small Auspiciousness (小吉 xiao ji)

The expected person comes in a happy time. This person belongs to Wood element and all directions. Generally in planning matters, use 1, 5, and 7. This position belongs to the liver and intestines. Helpful people are found in the Southwest. Avoid the East. Children, women and the six domestic animals are frightened.

Small Auspiciousness is most auspicious and prosperous. Your road is smooth. Spirits come announcing good news. Lost items are located in the Southwest. Travelers promptly arrive. Relations with others are extremely strong. Everything is harmonious. A sick person should pray to heaven.

6. Empty and Lost (空亡 kong wang)

News you expect does not come at this time. This position belongs to Earth element. Generally in planning matters, use 3, 6, and 9. This position belongs to the spleen and brain. Helpful people are found in the North. Watch out for the health of your children. Males feel pressure. The activities of females get no results.

Spirits are often unreasonable or perverse. Seeking wealth is without benefit. There is disaster for travelers. Lost items will not appear. Official activities bring punishment and damage. Sick people meet a dark ghost. To be secure and peaceful, get release from calamity by sacrifice and prayer.

Example: You arrive at the airport, but your ride is late to pick you up. You use Liu Ren to find out what is going on.

Today's time and date: May 10th, 2015, 2:30 pm

A. Start in Position One.

B. May 10th is in the column that says 3rd month at the top.
So we go to Position Three.
May 10th is the 22nd day of the 3rd month.
Start where we left off in Position Three and call that 1.

C. Count clockwise to the 22nd position from there: Position Six.
Start in Position Six and count for the hour.
Standard Time, 2:30 pm is the 8th hour.

D. Count 8 positions, with Position Six as the beginning, and end up in Position One.

This is the outcome:

Position Three is **Great Peace**
Read the text and apply it to the situation. Great Peace begins with "The person you expect has not left yet." Your flight had arrived early. You wait calmly for 30 minutes and your ride arrives, at what would've been on time.

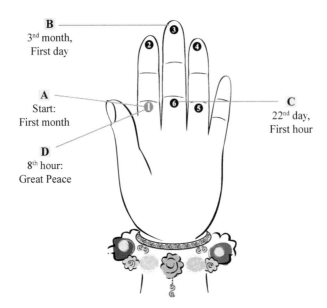

46

OMEN

OMENS

In Chinese almanacs, there are often listings of predictions based on omens. We include a few below. Have fun with it and don't take it seriously.

Omens from the Twitch of an Eye

Time	Eye	This is an omen of:
11 pm - 1 am Zi	Left	Meeting a benefactor
	Right	Having a good meal
1 - 3 am Chou	Left	Having anxiety
	Right	Someone thinking about you
3 - 5 am Yin	Left	Someone coming from afar
	Right	A happy matter arriving
5 - 7 am Mao	Left	The coming of an important guest
	Right	Something peaceful, safe and auspicious
7 - 9 am Chen	Left	A guest coming from afar
	Right	Injury or harm
9 - 11 am Si	Left	Having a good meal
	Right	Something inauspicious
11 am - 1 pm Wu	Left	Having a good meal
	Right	An inauspicious matter
1 - 3 pm Wei	Left	A lucky Star
	Right	Good luck, but small
3 - 5 pm Shen	Left	Money coming
	Right	Someone thinking of you romantically
5 - 7 pm You	Left	A guest coming
	Right	A guest arriving
7 - 9 pm Xu	Left	A guest arriving
	Right	A gathering or meeting
9 - 11 pm Hai	Left	A guest arriving
	Right	Gossip

Correct for *Daylight Savings Time*, if in use (subtract one hour from the current time).

Omens from Hiccoughs

Time	This is an omen of:
11 pm - 1 am Zi	A good meal and a happy dinner gathering
1 - 3 am Chou	Someone missing you; a guest coming to seek your help
3 - 5 am Yin	Someone missing you; a dining engagement
5 - 7 am Mao	Wealth and happiness; someone coming to ask about a matter
7 - 9 am Chen	A good meal; great good luck for everyone
9 - 11 am Si	A lucky person coming to seek wealth
11 am - 1 pm Wu	An important guest; someone wanting a dinner gathering
1 - 3 pm Wei	Someone wanting a meal; lucky activities
3 - 5 pm Shen	Nightmares; eating is not beneficial
5 - 7 pm You	Someone coming; someone asks about a matter
7 - 9 pm Xu	Someone missing you; a meeting brings benefit
9 - 11 pm Hai	Something frightens, but on the contrary, brings benefit

Correct for *Daylight Savings Time*, if in use (subtract one hour from the current time).

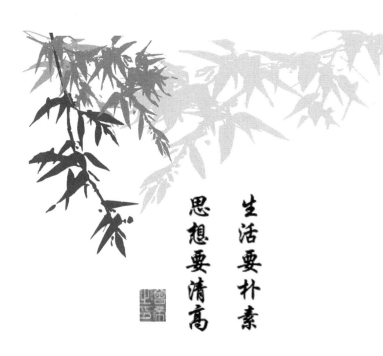

生活要朴素
思想要清高

Plain living and
higher thinking

THE YELLOW EMPEROR

THE YELLOW EMPEROR
IN THE FOUR SEASONS

黃帝四季詩

SPRING

AUTUMN

SUMMER

WINTER

There is a lifetime prediction commonly found in Chinese almanacs. Based on your season of birth, find your birth time.

The Yellow Emperor in the Four Seasons

Time of Birth		Season of Birth			
		Spring February 4th to May 4th	**Summer** May 5th to August 6th	**Autumn** August 7th to November 6th	**Winter** November 7th to February 3th
Zi	11p-1a	head	low abdomen	shoulders	low abdomen
Chou	1-3a	chest	hands	hands	knees
Yin	3-5a	feet	feet	knees	chest
Mao	5-7a	shoulders	shoulders	chest	shoulders
Chen	7-9a	knees	knees	feet	feet
Si	9-11a	hands	hands	hands	head
Wu	11a-1p	low abdomen	head	shoulders	hands
Wei	1-3p	hands	chest	chest	knees
Shen	3-5p	feet	feet	low abdomen	chest
You	5-7p	shoulders	shoulders	knees	shoulders
Xu	7-9p	knees	knees	feet	feet
Hai	9-11p	chest	chest	head	hands

Correct birth time for Daylight Saving Time, if used at the time of birth. If you were born in the Southern Hemisphere, switch the autumn and spring dates, as well as the summer and winter dates.

The Yellow Emperor in the Four Seasons

Born on the Yellow Emperor's Head means a lifetime of never having worries. Even petty people have riches and honor. Clothes and food naturally come around. Your position in society is elevated, and gentlemen are good at planning. Women go through life steadily and smoothly, marrying a talented and educated person.

Born on the Yellow Emperor's Hands means business capital is sufficient. Going out, you meet a benefactor. Inside the home, you have everything. Your early years are very steady and smooth. You accumulate many possessions. Wealth comes from every direction. When old, it is in your hands.

The Yellow Emperor in the Four Seasons

Born on the Yellow Emperor's Shoulders means a life of a million riches. You have wealth in your middle years. Children and grandchildren are plenty. Clothes and income at all times are good. In old age, you have fields in the village. Siblings are helpful. Your early life is bitter, but the later end is sweet.

Born on the Yellow Emperor's Chest means clothes and food are naturally ample. Experts in the pen and the sword are around you. There is music, song, and dance. Middle age brings good clothes and food. Later years are happy and prosperous. Joy, utmost honor, prosperity, and increased longevity add more blessings.

Born on the Yellow Emperor's Lower Abdomen, you were treasured by your parents. In middle age, clothes and food are good. When old you obtain gold. The family reputation is changing a lot. You are a noble person. Children and grandchildren must newly shine. Cultured and bright, they advance a lot.

Born on the Yellow Emperor's Knees means doing things is without benefit. In your early years, you toiled a lot, but did not lack clothes and food. Everyday, you travel on the road; you cannot avoid running back and forth. Old age is smooth, with honor and prosperity, but in middle age, hard work is extreme.

Born on the Yellow Emperor's Feet, practice moral teachings to avoid toil. A lifetime that is safe and sound, but unsuitable to reside in your ancestor's home. Women marry two husbands. Men have two wives. Search lonely mountain ranges. Leave your homeland to achieve good fortune.

FENG SHUI

FENG SHUI

Makes the Universe Work for You

 We live in a universe that is filled with different energies. Our planet rotates on its axis, creating cycles of day and night. The Earth also revolves around the sun in yearly cycles and is subject to various gravitational and magnetic fields. Our solar system is moving through space and is also subject to other forces in the universe. These physical forces and many different time cycles affects us profoundly. The Chinese have spent centuries observing the effects with their environment. This is the science and art of Feng Shui (Chinese geomancy).

Feng Shui uses observation, repeatable calculations and methodologies, and is based on the study of the environment, both inside and out of the house. Feng Shui can help you determine the best home to live in, which colors can enhance your home, the best bed positions for deep sleep, and how to change your business or home into a center of power. Feng Shui can help improve your health, your relationships and your prosperity. It is based on a complex calculation and observation of the environment, rather than a metaphysical reading relying on inspiration or intuition.

The American Feng Shui Institute publishes the annual Chinese Astrology and Feng Shui Guide so that both the Feng Shui professional and layperson can benefit from the knowledge of the incoming energy cycles and their influences. With this knowledge, one can adjust their environment to make it as harmonious as possible for the current year.

The following Sections contain the energy patterns for the current year with an analysis and remedy for each of the eight directions. For the nonprofessional, there is a Section on how to prepare your home for this reading. Please note that Feng Shui is a deep and complex science that requires many years to master. Preparing your home to receive the annual energy is one aspect that anyone can apply. A professional reading is recommended to anyone who wishes to receive the greatest benefits possible that Feng Shui can bring.

Preparing your home for a Feng Shui reading

The Floor Plan

The first requirement for preparing your home for a Feng Shui annual reading is to create a proportional floor plan. This plan can be hand drawn or be the original building plans, as long as the plan is proportionally correct. It is not necessary to draw in all your furniture except perhaps noting your bed and desk. It is important that you indicate where all window and door openings are.

**Example B
Floor Plan**

**Example A
Floor Plan**

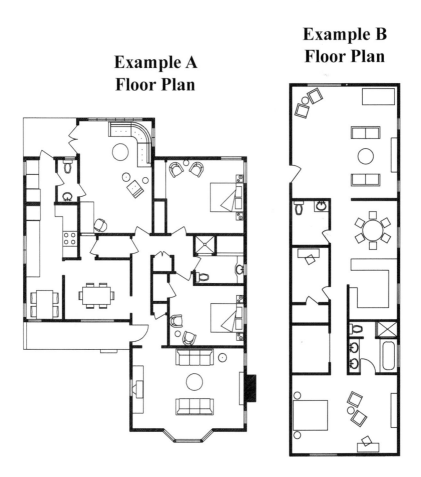

Preparing your home for a Feng Shui reading

Gridding The Floor Plan

Once you have your floor plan drawn, you then overlay a 9 - square grid. This grid is proportional to the floor plan. If it were a long and narrow house, so would the grid be long and narrow. You want to divide the floor plan into equal thirds both top to bottom and left to right as shown below:

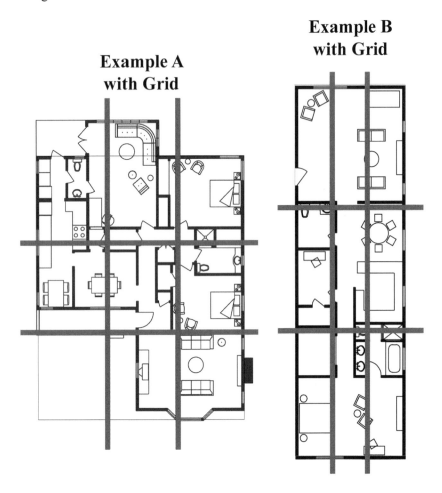

Example A with Grid

Example B with Grid

The Compass Reading

The next step is to determine the alignment of your house with the Earth magnetic fields by taking a compass reading. It is very important to take an accurate reading and not guess the orientation based on the direction of the sun or a map.

Why Do You Need To Use A Compass?

In Feng Shui, we look at the eight cardinal and inter-cardinal directions: East, Southeast, South, Southwest, West, Northwest, North, and Northeast when analyzing a home or building. Each of these directions hold unique significance to these building. If you do not use a compass to determine the correct orientation, you might completely misread your home. You cannot map the Qi within the building without an exact orientation. It is similar to finding your way out of a forest without a compass. You have a high probability of getting lost. Without a compass, it simply is not Feng Shui.

A Compass vs A Luopan

You can use any compass if you do not have a Luopan. The Luopan is simply a Chinese compass that helps determine the sitting direction of a building. It also contains a wealth of information on its dial that is used for more advanced applications. In recent years, Master Larry Sang simplified the traditional Luopan specifically for training Western students. Although it looks simple compared to an original Luopan, it has all the tools you need to accurately analyze a building. An important fact to remember about a Luopan is that it points to the South. The following information and instructions apply to a Luopan, however, if you are using a Western compass these concepts are easy to adapt.

SANG'S LUOPAN

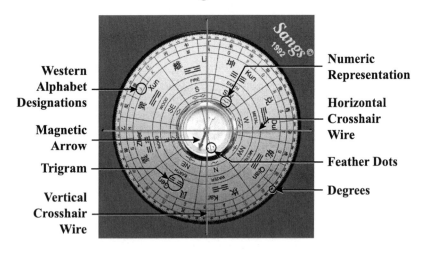

Western Alphabet Designations

Magnetic Arrow

Trigram

Vertical Crosshair Wire

Numeric Representation

Horizontal Crosshair Wire

Feather Dots

Degrees

Parts of Sang's Luopan

The Magnetic Arrow - The arrowhead points South rather than North. Western compasses point North.

The Feather Dots - (The twin dots at the center of the rotating dial). Always adjust the rotating (gold) dial to align the twin dots with the feather end of the arrow.

The Numeric Representations - The innermost ring has a dot pattern that represents the Trigram' numbers. For example Kun has two dots and Qian has six dots.

Crosshair Alignments - The red crosshairs designate the facing and sitting directions. Once the arrow is steady and the feather end is aligned over the North twin dots, you can determine the sitting direction and the facing direction.

The Eight Trigrams - The Eight Trigrams are the basis for orientation in Feng Shui and are shown on the Luopan with their perspective elements, symbols, and directions.

Western Alphabet Designations - Each Trigram is divided into three equal parts. These parts are shown with both their Chinese symbols and using the Western Alphabet.

The Degrees - Outermost on the dial are the Western compass degree in Arabic numerals.

General Guidelines for using the Luopan:

To use the Luopan or compass correctly, remember the following guidelines:

1. Always stand straight and upright.

2. Do not wear Metal jewelry or belt buckles that can skew the compass.

3. Avoid any electrical influences such as automobiles or electrical boxes.

4. Always stand parallel to the building.

5. Keep your feet square below you.

6. You can keep the Luopan in the lower box case to manage it better.

Taking a reading with the Luopan:

With the general guidelines for using a luopan in mind, now you ar ready to take a reading to determine which wall or corner of your home is located closest to the North.

1. Take your reading outside, standing parallel to your home with your back to it. Stand straight and hold the Luopan at waist level. Wait until the arrow ceases to quiver.

2. Slowly turn the center (gold) dial so that the North/feather dots aligh with the feather of the arrow. If using a Western compass, turn the compass so that the needle's arrow end aligns with North (between 337.5° - 22.5°).

3. Please take at lEast three separate readings from other positions. If you find that there is a discrepancy, take various readings at various locations until you are sure which one is correct. One direction should stand out as being correct.

4. Indicate on your floor plan which Section is North. Fill in the other directions as illustrated. Please note that North can lie in a corner Section.

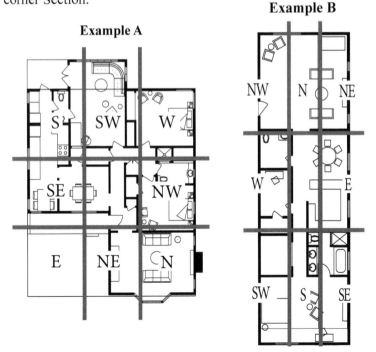

Example A

Example B

DIRECTIONS TO AVOID FOR CONSTRUCTION 2020

The Three Sha, Sui Po, and Tai Sui

* The **Three Sha** are in the **Southeast (Si)**,
  South (Wu), and **Southwest (Wei)** directions

* The **Sui Po** or **Year Breaker** is in the
  South (Wu) direction

* The **Tai Sui** is in the
  North (Zi) direction

Therefore, avoid using these directions:
Si, Bing, Wu, Ding, Wei, and Zi

Directions to Avoid

15° Direction	Degrees	45° Direction	Sang's Luopan Alpha Designation
Zi	352.5° -7.5°	N	a
Si		SE	k
Bing			l
Wu	142.5° -217.5°	S	m
Ding			n
Wei		SW	o

What should we avoid in these directions?

* New construction sitting in these directions (except North).
* Major renovation to buildings sitting in these directions (except North).
* Major renovation to this Section of the house, regardless of the sitting direction.
* Burial of the deceased in these directions.
* Digging or breaking of Earth in these directions.
* If digging cannot be avoided in any of these areas, then place a Metal wind chime outside between the house and the digging site.
* In addition, Horses or Rats born in the 1st, 5th, or 11th month of the lunar calendar should avoid attending funerals or burials.

FENG SHUI

2020

The Qi (energy) shift begins on
February 4th at 5:18 p.m.

SE **6** White	S **2** Black	SW **4** Green
E **5** Yellow	**7** Red	W **9** Purple
NE **1** White	N **3** Jade	NW **8** White

Qi Pattern

INTRODUCTION

While this diagram may look foreign to the beginner, it is essential information for the experienced Feng Shui practitioner. Each year the Qi pattern brings different effects. Some of these effects are quite auspicious and favorable and some may be inauspicious and not so favorable.

The effects of the 2020 energy pattern are analyzed for you in the following pages. Each analysis contains suggested remedies or enhancements for each Section. Remedies are recommended to reduce negative Qi. Enhancements are recommended to increase beneficial Qi. These remedies or enhancements consist of the five elements: Wood, Fire, Earth, Metal, and Water.

To use a remedy or enhancement, it must be placed inside the house within that particular Section. If more than one room exists within a Section, then each room needs to have its own remedy or enhancement. Any exceptions will be noted.

Feng Shui

FENG SHUI 2020

SE **6** White	**S** **2** Black	**SW** **4** Green
E **5** Yellow	Fighting Star *Po Jun* **7** Red	**W** **9** Purple
NE **1** White	**N** **3** Jade	**NW** **8** White

The Center Section

Center

Analysis

Last year (2019), the **8 White Zuo Fu Star** visited the center. Which suggessted that Mountain above Mountain forms a hexagram 52, Gen Gua. The meaning of this hexagram is "Keeping still; impediment." The world was entering an era of "slower growth" and economic recovery would be slow and painful.

In 2020, the **7 Red Po Jun Fighting Star** visits the center. We are currently in Period 8, so the 8 White (Earth element) Star is in the center, and is productive to 7 Red Po Jun (Metal). From this, we can predict that this year the world will enter another era of "increased fighting and conflict." Economic recovery may still be slow and painful. The weakness in the labor market will persist for longer than we would like.

Together 8 White and 7 Red form Sun Hexagram 41 in the Yi Jing. The meaning of this hexagram is "to decrease" or "to reduce." Decrease does not always mean something bad. Increase and decrease come in their own time. What matters here is to understand this moment in time and not cover up poverty with empty pretense.

Feng Shui

FENG SHUI 2020

SE	S	SW
6 White	**2** Black	**4** Green
E Disaster Star *Lian Zhen* **5** Yellow	**7** Red	**W** **9** Purple
NE **1** White	**N** **3** Jade	**NW** **8** White

The East Section

East

Situation
Doors, bedrooms, or study rooms in the East Section.

Analysis
This year the **5 Yellow Lian Zhen Disaster Star** falls in the East. This is a sign for potential delays, obstacles, fires, lawsuits, sickness, and casualties. The 5 Yellow Star is an Earth element The East Section is the home of the 3 Jade Lu Cun Star which is related to gossip, lawsuits and robbery. The Lu Cun Star is Wood element. Wood dominates Earth, so the East Section is definitely not an auspicious area. If unfortunately the main entrance or bedroom is located in this Section and no remedy is applied, an unexpected casualty is possible. It is advisable to avoid spending a lot of time in this area. In the East Section, ground digging should especially be avoided to prevent the occurrences of misfortune.

Remedy
To reduce the potential negative effects, use Metal element as a remedy in this Section. A Metal remedy can consist of Metal décor such as a sculpture. An ornament that has moving Metal parts is preferable, such as a grandfather clock.

After Remedy
Beneficial for business expansion and promotion, as well as for people who work in speech-related professions such as sales, singers, and fortune tellers.

Caution
Do not allow construction or ground digging.

Feng Shui

FENG SHUI

2020

SE Fortune Star *Wu Qu* **6** White	**S** **2** Black	**SW** **4** Green
E **5** Yellow	**7** Red	**W** **9** Purple
NE **1** White	**N** **3** Jade	**NW** **8** White

The Southeast Section

Southeast

Situation

Doors, bedrooms, or study rooms in the Southeast Section.

Analysis

The **6 White Fortune Star** visits the Southeast in 2020. The 6 Fortune Star is a sharp yang Metal. The Southeast Section is the home of the 4 Green Wen Qu Literary Star, which is Wood element. The combination of the Wood of 4 Green and the Metal of 6 White creates a domination relationship. This makes the Southeast Section not beneficial for artists, writers and people working in entertainment business. There is also potential injury to the thighs or pain at the waist can occur. A female whose bedroom is in this Section easily receives some kind of cheating romance. Still, you can make use of the Water element to change the above mentioned negative Qi into positive Qi. However, under influence of the inauspicious Jie Sha (Robbery) Star, be on guard for unexpected casualties or break-ins. Avoid ground digging.

Caution

Not beneficial for artists, writers and people working in the entertainment business. Easy to expeirence unhappiness in romance.

Remedy

Use Water element as a remedy in this Section. A fountain or aquarium in the Southeast will help to change the poison into medicine.

After Remedy

It will bring strong romance Qi (Peach Blossoms) and good results in academia, for students, writers, and people working in the entertainment industry.

FENG SHUI 2020

SE ☰ **6** White	**S** Sickness Star *Ju Men* ☷ **2** Black	**SW** ☷ **4** Green
E ☳ **5** Yellow	 **7** Red	**W** ☵ **9** Purple
NE ☶ **1** White	**N** ☲ **3** Jade	**NW** ☴ **8** White

The South Section

South

Situation
Doors, bedrooms, or study rooms in the South Section.

Analysis
The **2 Black Ju Men Star** visits the South this year. 2 Black is Earth element. The South is associated with Fire. Fire feeds 2 Black Earth, strengthening the illness Qi strong. The Disaster Sha and Da Hao inauspicious Stars are also in the South; therefore, if the main entrance falls in this Section you should be careful of conflict with others or money loss and be on guard against unexpected casualty because of sex. Therefore, this area is not good for your main entrance, bedroom or for lots of activity. If a female's bedroom is in the South, it is particularly easy to be stricken by illness. Pregnant women should take every precaution against miscarriage by avoiding spending time here or using a door in the South.

Remedy
Use Metal element in your décor to reduce the unhealthy 2 Black Sickness energy.

Caution
Pregnant women should avoid using the South Section. Avoid ground digging due to the Sui Sha Star locates in this sector.

FENG SHUI

2020

SE	S	SW
6 White	**2** Black	
E		W
5 Yellow	**7** Red	**9** Purple
NE	N	NW
1 White	**3** Jade	**8** White

The Southwest Section

74

Southwest

Situation
Doors, bedrooms, or study rooms in the Southwest Section.

Analysis
This year the **4 Green Literary Star** visits the Southwest. 4 Green is related to Wood. The Southwest is Earth element. Wood dominates Earth. The auspicious Star Lu Cun(祿存) gives the Southwest strong money luck and Peach Blossomss (romance and social relationships), especially for males to attract a female. It is also good for artists and people in entertainment industry.

Remedy
Put Water in a Metal container in the Southwest to cancel out the domination relationship and enhance the 4 Green Literary Wen Qu Star.

Benefits
Beneficial for writers, artists, public relationships, or entertainment-related businesses, such as bars, nightclubs and casinos. Strong for Peach Blossoms.

Caution
Be wary of excessive Peach Blossoms that may lead to problems for married couples.

Feng Shui

FENG SHUI

2020

SE	S	SW
6 White	**2** Black	**4** Green
E **5** Yellow	**7** Red	**W** Celebration Star *You Bi* **9** Purple
NE **1** White	**N** **3** Jade	**NW** **8** White

The West Section

West

Situation

Doors, bedrooms, or study rooms in the West Section.

Analysis

The **9 Purple Celebration Star** is in the West this year. This Celebration Star gathers together with yearly auspicious Stars such as the Tian De, and Tian Xi, making this Section strong in Peach Blossoms and money luck. Make use of this Section, it will be quite beneficial for the self-employed to expand their business while salaried workers easily gain promotions.

Benefits

Beneficial for expanding business, gaining recognition and welcoming in new family members. Strong Peach Blossoms.

Caution

Avoid ground digging or construction.

Feng Shui

FENG SHUI 2020

SE **6** White	**S** **2** Black	**SW** **4** Green
E **5** Yellow	**7** Red	**W** **9** Purple
NE **1** White	**N** **3** Jade	**NW** Money Star *Zuo Fu* **8** White

The Northwest Section

Northwest

Situation
Doors, bedrooms, or study rooms in the Northwest Section.

Analysis
The **8 White Zuo Fu Money Star** is in the Northwest Section this year. It brings fame and wealth. The 8 White Zuo Fu Money Star is Earth. The Northwest is the home of the 6 White Fortune Star, which is Metal element. The productive relationship of Earth and Metal make this Section quite excellent. In Feng Shui, 6 White and 8 White together means "when Heaven comes to Mountain, a billionaire is made". These two White Fortune Stars together make the Northwest a wealth-making and power-enhancing Section.

Benefits
Beneficial for politicians to extend power and businessmen to expand their business.

Caution
Avoid ground digging to prevent conflicts; arguments and misunderstandings are easily aroused between young and old people.

Feng Shui

FENG SHUI

2020

SE	S	SW
☷ **6**	☵ **2**	☴ **4**
White	Black	Green
E		W
☶ **5**	**7**	☳ **9**
Yellow	Red	Purple
NE	N Lo Cun Star **3** Jade	NW
☷ **1**		☰ **8**
White		White

The North Section

North

Situation
Doors, bedrooms, or study rooms in the North Section.

Analysis
The **3 Jade Lu Cun Star** falls into the North. This 3 Jade Star is Wood element, it is associated with aggression, expansion, gossip and legal problems. The North is the home of the 1 White Fortune Star, and it is Water element. 1 White (Water) and the 3 Jade (Wood) are in an engendering relationship. 1 White and 3 Jade in the North make this Section very strong for self-motivation and moving forward. However, a number of inauspicious Stars gather in the North; therefore, it is inadvisable to have moving Water in this Section to prevent the occurrence of misfortunes such as lawsuits, break-ins or robbery.

Benefits
Beneficial for attorneys, law firms, brokers, and sales.

Caution
No moving Water in the North.

Feng Shui

FENG SHUI 2020

SE	S	SW
6 White	**2** Black	**4** Green
E **5** Yellow	**7** Red	**W** **9** Purple
NE Fortune Star *Tan Lang* **1** White	**N** **3** Jade	**NW** **8** White

The Northeast Section

Northeast

Situation

Doors, bedrooms, or study rooms in the Northeast Section.

Analysis

The **1 White Fortune Star** visits the Northeast Section this year. 1 White is Water element. This Star represents wealth and Peach Blossoms. The Northeast is the home of the 8 White Zuo Fu Money Star which also brings fame and wealth. Its element is Earth. 1 white and 8 white have a domination relationship. Even though these two fortune and money Star are hand in hand, there are also inauspicious Stars in this Section. Because of this, it is not advisable to do any kind of risky investments or overwork. No doubt, this Section will produce a lot of wealth opportunities. Be cautious, as it is easy to experience sex scandals and stricken by illness too.

Caution

Not beneficial for over-aggressive expansion. Stay away from extramarital affairs and avoid visiting the sick.

Remedy

Use Fire element as a remedy here. A Fire remedy can be a red light bulb, a lamp with a red shade, or any red color item. The related Fire colors of maroon, purple, or fuchsia may also be used.

Remedy

Always keep this area clean and bright. Put in Metal element to change the domination relationship into a productive relationship.

Feng Shui

活在当下

花开堪折直须折

莫待无花空折枝

Live in the present,
Don't wait until tomorrow;
pick your roses today

DAY SELECTION

DAY SELECTION

Introduction to Day Selection

Day Selection has been used for a long time in China. Every year, almanacs would be published giving the best days for important activities, as well as days to avoid. It is thought that a positive outcome is more likely when an activity is begun on an auspicious day. In English, we talk abut getting things off to a good Start, but have no particular methodology to do this.

There are three aspects to selecting a good day: picking a day that is good for the activity, avoiding a day that is bad for the activity, and picking a day that is not bad for the person(s) involved. In the calendar pages that follow, each day will list two or three activities that are auspicious or inauspicious on that day. If you wanted to pick a date to get married, you would first look for the days that were considered good for weddings. In addition, you need to check the birth information of the bride and groom. If the bride is a Rabbit and the groom is a Rat, then you also need to avoid any days that say Bad for Rat or Bad for Rabbit, even if they are good for weddings in general.

In addition, there are some days that are not good for any important activity. Usually this is because the energy of heaven and Earth is too strong or inharmonious on those days.

Day Selection is used for the first day of an activity. It does not affect a continued activity. For example, you should begin construction on a day that is good for ground breaking, but it is not a problem if the construction is continued through a day that is bad for ground breaking. The construction need not be stopped.

On the next page are definitions of the various activities included in Master Sang's Day Selection Calendar.

CALENDAR TERMINOLOGY KEY

Animals:
Generally a bad day for a person born in the year of the animal listed. Even if an activity is listed as beneficial for that day, it will usually not be beneficial for that animal.

*Begin Mission:
Beginning a new position, mission, or assignment.

Burial:
Burial.

*Business:
Trade or business.

*Buy Property:
Purchasing real estate.

*Construction:
Begin work on buildings, roads, etc.

*Contracts:
Signing or entering into a contract, commitment, or agreement.

Don't Do Important Things:
A bad day for most activities.

Fix House:
Repairing the inside or outside of the house. Also for installing major appliances, such as the stove or oven.

Funeral:
Funerals.

*Grand Opening:
Opening a new business, restaurant, etc. Opening ceremonies for a new event.

Ground Breaking:
Beginning construction or disturbing the Earth.

Ground Digging:
Unearth or excavate the Earth with a shovel or spade to remove material or plants.

Hunting:
To chase wild animals for the purpose of catching or killing.

Lawsuit:
Filing a lawsuit or going to court.

*Moving:
Moving or changing residences.

Planting:
Gardening or planting.

Prayer:
Praying for blessings or happiness.

School:
Admissions into a new school.

Surgery:
Medical treatment or operation.

*Travel:
Going out or beginning a trip.

*Wedding:
Marriage ceremonies or becoming engaged to be married.

Worship:
Rituals, rites, ceremonies, offering sacrifices, or honoring ancestors or the dead.

Most Activities:
Includes all activities marked. (*)

S	M	T	W	T	F	S
			1	2	3	4
5	6	7	8	9	10	11
12	13	14	15	16	17	18
19	20	21	22	23	24	25
26	27	28	29	30	31	

January 2020

unfavorable for:

Day	Activities	Unfavorable for
Wed 1	**Good for:** worship, prayer *Bad for: most activities*	*Rooster*
Thu 2	**Good for:** moving, wedding, grand opening *Bad for: hunting, surgery*	*Dog*
Fri 3	⊖ **DON'T DO IMPORTANT THINGS** ⊖	*Pig*
Sat 4	⊖ **DON'T DO IMPORTANT THINGS** ⊖	*Rat*
Sun 5	**Good for:** prayer, house cleaning *Bad for: wedding, grand opening*	*Ox*
Mon 6	**Good for:** begin mission, contract, planting *Bad for: lawsuit, surgery*	*Tiger*
Tue 7	**Good for:** most activities *Bad for: funeral, lawsuit*	*Rabbit*
Wed 8	**Good for:** prayer, planting *Bad for: lawsuit, contract*	*Dragon*
Thu 9	**Good for:** worship, prayer *Bad for: surgery, lawsuit*	*Snake*
Fri 10	**Good for:** prayer, house cleaning *Bad for: wedding, grand opening*	*Horse*
Sat 11	**Good for:** worship, prayer *Bad for: most activities*	*Sheep*
Sun 12	**Good for:** planting, worship *Bad for: contract, business*	*Monkey*
Mon 13	**Good for:** most activities *Bad for: burial, ground digging*	*Rooster*
Tue 14	⊖ **DON'T DO IMPORTANT THINGS** ⊖	*Dog*
Wed 15	⊖ **DON'T DO IMPORTANT THINGS** ⊖	*Pig*

Thu **16**	**Good for:** prayer, planting *Bad for: lawsuit, contract*	*Rat*
Fri **17**	⊖ **DON'T DO IMPORTANT THINGS** ⊖	*Ox*
Sat **18**	**Good for:** business, begin mission, contract *Bad for: lawsuit, ground digging*	*Tiger*
Sun **19**	**Good for:** moving, wedding, grand opening *Bad for: hunting, surgery*	*Rabbit*
Mon **20**	**Good for:** prayer, planting *Bad for: lawsuit, contract*	*Dragon*
Tue **21**	**Good for:** fix house, house cleaning *Bad for: most activities*	*Snake*
Wed **22**	**Good for:** prayer, house cleaning *Bad for: wedding, grand opening*	*Horse*
Thu **23**	**Good for:** contract, business, buy property *Bad for: moving, travel, fix house*	*Sheep*
Fri **24**	**Good for:** prayer, house cleaning *Bad for: wedding, grand opening*	*Monkey*
Sat **25**	**Good for:** planting, worship *Bad for: contract, business*	*Rooster*
Sun **26**	**Good for:** worship, prayer *Bad for: surgery, lawsuit*	*Dog*
Mon **27**	⊖ **DON'T DO IMPORTANT THINGS** ⊖	*Pig*
Tue **28**	**Good for:** wedding, contract, grand opening *Bad for: burial, funeral*	*Rat*
Wed **29**	⊖ **DON'T DO IMPORTANT THINGS** ⊖	*Ox*
Thu **30**	**Good for:** worship, prayer *Bad for: most activities*	*Tiger*
Fri **31**	**Good for:** grand opening, wedding, contract *Bad for: hunting, surgery*	*Rabbit*

S	M	T	W	T	F	S
						1
2	3	4	5	6	7	8
9	10	11	12	13	14	15
16	17	18	19	20	21	22
23	24	25	26	27	28	29

February 2020

unfavorable for:

Sat 1	**Good for:** prayer, house cleaning	*Bad for: wedding, grand opening*	*Dragon*
Sun 2	**Good for:** moving, wedding, grand opening	*Bad for: hunting, surgery*	*Snake*
Mon 3	**Good for:** school, worship	*Bad for: wedding, grand opening, travel*	*Horse*
Tue 4	**Good for:** worship, prayer	*Bad for: most activities*	*Sheep*
Wed 5	**Good for:** contract, construction, buy property	*Bad for: funeral, lawsuit*	*Monkey*
Thu 6	**Good for:** wedding, grand opening, business	*Bad for: burial, funeral*	*Rooster*
Fri 7	**Good for:** worship, prayer	*Bad for: most activities*	*Dog*
Sat 8	**Good for:** prayer, house cleaning	*Bad for: wedding, grand opening*	*Pig*
Sun 9	⊖ **DON'T DO IMPORTANT THINGS** ⊖		*Rat*
Mon 10	**Good for:** planting, worship	*Bad for: contract, business*	*Ox*
Tue 11	⊖ **DON'T DO IMPORTANT THINGS** ⊖		*Tiger*
Wed 12	**Good for:** fix house, house cleaning	*Bad for: most activities*	*Rabbit*
Thu 13	**Good for:** most activities	*Bad for: funeral, lawsuit*	*Dragon*
Fri 14	**Good for:** wedding, contract, grand opening	*Bad for: funeral, lawsuit*	*Snake*

Sat **15**	**Good for:** planting, worship **Bad for:** *contract, business*	*Horse*
Sun **16**	**Good for:** worship, prayer **Bad for:** *most activities*	*Sheep*
Mon **17**	**Good for:** school, worship **Bad for:** *wedding, grand opening, travel*	*Monkey*
Tue **18**	**Good for:** most activities **Bad for:** *burial, ground digging*	*Rooster*
Wed **19**	**Good for:** grand opening, wedding, contract **Bad for:** *hunting, surgery*	*Dog*
Thu **20**	**Good for:** fix house, house cleaning **Bad for:** *most activities*	*Pig*
Fri **21**	⊖ **DON'T DO IMPORTANT THINGS** ⊖	*Rat*
Sat **22**	**Good for:** worship, prayer **Bad for:** *contract, business*	*Ox*
Sun **23**	⊖ **DON'T DO IMPORTANT THINGS** ⊖	*Tiger*
Mon **24**	**Good for:** most activities **Bad for:** *funeral, lawsuit*	*Rabbit*
Tue **25**	**Good for:** worship, prayer **Bad for:** *most activities*	*Dragon*
Wed **26**	**Good for:** grand opening, wedding, contract **Bad for:** *hunting, surgery*	*Snake*
Thu **27**	**Good for:** school, worship **Bad for:** *wedding, grand opening, travel*	*Horse*
Fri **28**	**Good for:** prayer, house cleaning **Bad for:** *wedding, grand opening*	*Sheep*
Sat **29**	**Good for:** grand opening, wedding, contract **Bad for:** *hunting, surgery*	*Monkey*

S	M	T	W	T	F	S
1	2	3	4	5	6	7
8	9	10	11	12	13	14
15	16	17	18	19	20	21
22	23	24	25	26	27	28
29	30	31				

March 2020

unfavorable for:

Sun **1**		**Good for:** contract, construction, buy property ***Bad for:*** *funeral, lawsuit*	*Rooster*
Mon **2**		**Good for:** worship, prayer ***Bad for:*** *most activities*	*Dog*
Tue **3**		**Good for:** prayer, house cleaning ***Bad for:*** *wedding, grand opening*	*Pig*
Wed **4**		⊖ **DON'T DO IMPORTANT THINGS** ⊖	*Rat*
Thu **5**		**Good for:** most activities ***Bad for:*** *burial, funeral*	*Ox*
Fri **6**		**Good for:** worship, prayer ***Bad for:*** *most activities*	*Tiger*
Sat **7**		⊖ **DON'T DO IMPORTANT THINGS** ⊖	*Rabbit*
Sun **8**		**Good for:** prayer, house cleaning ***Bad for:*** *wedding, grand opening*	*Dragon*
Mon **9**		**Good for:** most activities ***Bad for:*** *burial, ground digging*	*Snake*
Tue **10**		**Good for:** worship, prayer ***Bad for:*** *most activities*	*Horse*
Wed **11**		**Good for:** most activities ***Bad for:*** *funeral, lawsuit*	*Sheep*
Thu **12**		**Good for:** planting, worship ***Bad for:*** *contract, business*	*Monkey*
Fri **13**		**Good for:** prayer, house cleaning ***Bad for:*** *wedding, grand opening*	*Rooster*
Sat **14**		**Good for:** wedding, grand opening, business ***Bad for:*** *funeral, lawsuit*	*Dog*
Sun **15**		**Good for:** contract, business, buy property ***Bad for:*** *moving, travel, fix house*	*Pig*

92

Mon **16**	⊖ **DON'T DO IMPORTANT THINGS** ⊖	*Rat*
Tue **17**	**Good for:** most activities *Bad for: burial, funeral*	*Ox*
Wed **18**	**Good for:** worship, prayer *Bad for: most activities*	*Tiger*
Thu **19**	⊖ **DON'T DO IMPORTANT THINGS** ⊖	*Rabbit*
Fri **20**	**Good for:** fix house, house cleaning *Bad for: most activities*	*Dragon*
Sat **21**	**Good for:** school , worship *Bad for: wedding, grand opening, travel*	*Snake*
Sun **22**	**Good for:** worship, prayer *Bad for: contract, business*	*Horse*
Mon **23**	**Good for:** most activities *Bad for: funeral, lawsuit*	*Sheep*
Tue **24**	**Good for:** begin mission, contract, planting *Bad for: lawsuit, surgery*	*Monkey*
Wed **25**	**Good for:** wedding, grand opening, business *Bad for: burial, ground digging*	*Rooster*
Thu **26**	**Good for:** school , worship *Bad for: wedding, grand opening, travel*	*Dog*
Fri **27**	**Good for:** contract, business, buy property *Bad for: burial, ground digging*	*Pig*
Sat **28**	⊖ **DON'T DO IMPORTANT THINGS** ⊖	*Rat*
Sun **29**	**Good for:** most activities *Bad for: funeral, lawsuit*	*Ox*
Mon **30**	**Good for:** worship, prayer *Bad for: most activities*	*Tiger*
Tue **31**	⊖ **DON'T DO IMPORTANT THINGS** ⊖	*Rabbit*

April 2020

S	M	T	W	T	F	S
			1	2	3	4
5	6	7	8	9	10	11
12	13	14	15	16	17	18
19	20	21	22	23	24	25
26	27	28	29	30		

unfavorable for:

Date		Unfavorable
Wed 1	**Good for:** most activities — **Bad for:** *funeral, lawsuit*	*Dragon*
Thu 2	**Good for:** begin mission, grand opening, business — **Bad for:** *funeral, lawsuit*	*Snake*
Fri 3	**Good for:** worship, prayer — **Bad for:** *most activities*	*Horse*
Sat 4	**Good for:** most activities — **Bad for:** *hunting, surgery*	*Sheep*
Sun 5	**Good for:** begin mission, contract, planting — **Bad for:** *burial, funeral*	*Monkey*
Mon 6	**Good for:** worship, prayer — **Bad for:** *most activities*	*Rooster*
Tue 7	**Good for:** worship, prayer — **Bad for:** *most activities*	*Dog*
Wed 8	**Good for:** prayer, house cleaning — **Bad for:** *wedding, grand opening*	*Pig*
Thu 9	⊖ **DON'T DO IMPORTANT THINGS** ⊖	*Rat*
Fri 10	**Good for:** school, worship — **Bad for:** *wedding, grand opening, travel*	*Ox*
Sat 11	**Good for:** worship, prayer — **Bad for:** *surgery, lawsuit*	*Tiger*
Sun 12	**Good for:** worship, prayer — **Bad for:** *burial, ground digging*	*Rabbit*
Mon 13	⊖ **DON'T DO IMPORTANT THINGS** ⊖	*Dragon*
Tue 14	**Good for:** most activities — **Bad for:** *funeral, lawsuit*	*Snake*
Wed 15	**Good for:** wedding, grand opening, business — **Bad for:** *burial, lawsuit*	*Horse*

Thu **16**	**Good for:** worship, prayer *Bad for: most activities*	*Sheep*
Fri **17**	**Good for:** wedding, contract, grand opening *Bad for: funeral, lawsuit*	*Monkey*
Sat **18**	**Good for:** school, worship *Bad for: wedding, grand opening, travel*	*Rooster*
Sun **19**	**Good for:** worship, prayer *Bad for: most activities*	*Dog*
Mon **20**	**Good for:** prayer, house cleaning *Bad for: most activities*	*Pig*
Tue **21**	⊖ **DON'T DO IMPORTANT THINGS** ⊖	*Rat*
Wed **22**	**Good for:** school, worship *Bad for: wedding, grand opening, travel*	*Ox*
Thu **23**	**Good for:** burial, ground digging *Bad for: wedding, grand opening, contract*	*Tiger*
Fri **24**	**Good for:** wedding, grand opening, contract *Bad for: burial, ground digging*	*Rabbit*
Sat **25**	⊖ **DON'T DO IMPORTANT THINGS** ⊖	*Dragon*
Sun **26**	**Good for:** prayer, house cleaning *Bad for: most activities*	*Snake*
Mon **27**	**Good for:** most activities *Bad for: burial, funeral*	*Horse*
Tue **28**	**Good for:** worship, prayer *Bad for: most activities*	*Sheep*
Wed **29**	**Good for:** most activities *Bad for: hunting, surgery*	*Monkey*
Thu **30**	**Good for:** school, worship *Bad for: most activities*	*Rooster*

May 2020

unfavorable for:

Date		Entry	Zodiac
Fri **1**		**Good for:** prayer, house cleaning ***Bad for:*** *most activities*	*Dog*
Sat **2**		**Good for:** worship, prayer ***Bad for:*** *wedding, grand opening, contract*	*Pig*
Sun **3**		⊖ **DON'T DO IMPORTANT THINGS** ⊖	*Rat*
Mon **4**		**Good for:** begin mission, school, planting ***Bad for:*** *funeral, lawsuit*	*Ox*
Tue **5**		**Good for:** worship, prayer ***Bad for:*** *most activities*	*Tiger*
Wed **6**		**Good for:** most activities ***Bad for:*** *burial, funeral*	*Rabbit*
Thu **7**		**Good for:** wedding, grand opening, contract ***Bad for:*** *hunting, surgery*	*Dragon*
Fri **8**		⊖ **DON'T DO IMPORTANT THINGS** ⊖	*Snake*
Sat **9**		**Good for:** worship, prayer ***Bad for:*** *most activities*	*Horse*
Sun **10**		**Good for:** grand opening, begin mission, contract ***Bad for:*** *hunting, surgery*	*Sheep*
Mon **11**		**Good for:** school, worship ***Bad for:*** *most activities*	*Monkey*
Tue **12**		**Good for:** wedding, grand opening, business ***Bad for:*** *burial, funeral*	*Rooster*
Wed **13**		**Good for:** prayer, worship ***Bad for:*** *most activities*	*Dog*
Thu **14**		**Good for:** begin mission, school, planting ***Bad for:*** *most activities*	*Pig*
Fri **15**		⊖ **DON'T DO IMPORTANT THINGS** ⊖	*Rat*

Sat	**16**	**Good for:** worship, prayer *Bad for: most activities*	Ox
Sun	**17**	**Good for:** most activities *Bad for: hunting, surgery*	Tiger
Mon	**18**	**Good for:** wedding, grand opening, business *Bad for: burial, funeral*	Rabbit
Tue	**19**	**Good for:** school, worship *Bad for: most activities*	Dragon
Wed	**20**	● **DON'T DO IMPORTANT THINGS** ●	Snake
Thu	**21**	**Good for:** worship, prayer *Bad for: most activities*	Horse
Fri	**22**	**Good for:** wedding, grand opening, business *Bad for: funeral, lawsuit*	Sheep
Sat	**23**	**Good for:** most activities *Bad for: burial, ground digging*	Monkey
Sun	**24**	**Good for:** school, worship, prayer *Bad for: most activities*	Rooster
Mon	**25**	**Good for:** worship, prayer *Bad for: most activities*	Dog
Tue	**26**	**Good for:** worship, prayer *Bad for: wedding, grand opening*	Pig
Wed	**27**	● **DON'T DO IMPORTANT THINGS** ●	Rat
Thu	**28**	**Good for:** burial, funeral *Bad for: wedding, buy property, begin mission*	Ox
Fri	**29**	**Good for:** worship, prayer *Bad for: most activities*	Tiger
Sat	**30**	**Good for:** most activities *Bad for: funeral, lawsuit*	Rabbit
Sun	**31**	**Good for:** prayer, planting *Bad for: lawsuit, contract*	Dragon

S	M	T	W	T	F	S
	1	2	3	4	5	6
7	8	9	10	11	12	13
14	15	16	17	18	19	20
21	22	23	24	25	26	27
28	29	30				

June 2020

unfavorable for:

Mon 1	⊖ **DON'T DO IMPORTANT THINGS** ⊖	*Snake*
Tue 2	**Good for:** contract, construction, buy property *Bad for: funeral, lawsuit*	*Horse*
Wed 3	**Good for:** most activities *Bad for: burial, funeral*	*Sheep*
Thu 4	**Good for:** worship, prayer *Bad for: most activities*	*Monkey*
Fri 5	**Good for:** worship, prayer *Bad for: most activities*	*Rooster*
Sat 6	**Good for:** contract, construction, buy property *Bad for: funeral, lawsuit*	*Dog*
Sun 7	**Good for:** prayer, planting *Bad for: lawsuit, contract*	*Pig*
Mon 8	⊖ **DON'T DO IMPORTANT THINGS** ⊖	*Rat*
Tue 9	**Good for:** wedding, grand opening, business *Bad for: burial, funeral*	*Ox*
Wed 10	**Good for:** most activities *Bad for: hunting, surgery*	*Tiger*
Thu 11	**Good for:** worship, prayer *Bad for: most activities*	*Rabbit*
Fri 12	**Good for:** wedding, grand opening, business *Bad for: funeral, lawsuit*	*Dragon*
Sat 13	**Good for:** worship, prayer *Bad for: most activities*	*Snake*
Sun 14	⊖ **DON'T DO IMPORTANT THINGS** ⊖	*Horse*
Mon 15	**Good for:** worship, prayer *Bad for: most activities*	*Sheep*

Tue **16**	**Good for:** most activities ***Bad for:*** *hunting, surgery*	*Monkey*
Wed **17**	**Good for:** worship, prayer ***Bad for:*** *most activities*	*Rooster*
Thu **18**	**Good for:** contract, construction, buy property ***Bad for:*** *funeral, lawsuit*	*Dog*
Fri **19**	**Good for:** house cleaning, prayer ***Bad for:*** *most activities*	*Pig*
Sat **20**	⬤ **DON'T DO IMPORTANT THINGS** ⬤	*Rat*
Sun **21**	**Good for:** most activities ***Bad for:*** *hunting, surgery*	*Ox*
Mon **22**	**Good for:** moving, wedding, grand opening ***Bad for:*** *burial, funeral*	*Tiger*
Tue **23**	**Good for:** worship, prayer ***Bad for:*** *most activities*	*Rabbit*
Wed **24**	**Good for:** wedding, grand opening, business ***Bad for:*** *burial, funeral*	*Dragon*
Thu **25**	⬤ **DON'T DO IMPORTANT THINGS** ⬤	*Snake*
Fri **26**	⬤ **DON'T DO IMPORTANT THINGS** ⬤	*Horse*
Sat **27**	**Good for:** worship, prayer ***Bad for:*** *contract, business*	*Sheep*
Sun **28**	**Good for:** wedding, grand opening, business ***Bad for:*** *funeral, lawsuit*	*Monkey*
Mon **29**	**Good for:** school, worship ***Bad for:*** *wedding, grand opening, travel*	*Rooster*
Tue **30**	**Good for:** worship, prayer ***Bad for:*** *most activities*	*Dog*

S	M	T	W	T	F	S
			1	2	3	4
5	6	7	8	9	10	11
12	13	14	15	16	17	18
19	20	21	22	23	24	25
26	27	28	29	30	31	

July 2020

unfavorable for:

Date	Activity	Unfavorable
Wed **1**	**Good for:** prayer, house cleaning *Bad for: most activities*	*Pig*
Thu **2**	⛔ **DON'T DO IMPORTANT THINGS** ⛔	*Rat*
Fri **3**	**Good for:** most activities *Bad for: hunting, surgery*	*Ox*
Sat **4**	**Good for:** wedding, grand opening, business *Bad for: burial, funeral*	*Tiger*
Sun **5**	**Good for:** worship, prayer *Bad for: wedding, grand opening*	*Rabbit*
Mon **6**	**Good for:** prayer, house cleaning *Bad for: most activities*	*Dragon*
Tue **7**	**Good for:** wedding, contract, construction *Bad for: funeral, lawsuit*	*Snake*
Wed **8**	**Good for:** school, worship *Bad for: most activities*	*Horse*
Thu **9**	⛔ **DON'T DO IMPORTANT THINGS** ⛔	*Sheep*
Fri **10**	**Good for:** begin mission, school, grand opening *Bad for: funeral, lawsuit*	*Monkey*
Sat **11**	**Good for:** most activities *Bad for: hunting, surgery*	*Rooster*
Sun **12**	**Good for:** begin mission, contract, planting *Bad for: lawsuit, surgery*	*Dog*
Mon **13**	**Good for:** worship, prayer *Bad for: most activities*	*Pig*
Tue **14**	⛔ **DON'T DO IMPORTANT THINGS** ⛔	*Rat*
Wed **15**	**Good for:** moving, travel, fix house *Bad for: wedding, grand opening, business*	*Ox*

100

Thu **16**	**Good for:** worship, prayer *Bad for: wedding, contract, grand opening*	*Tiger*
Fri **17**	**Good for:** prayer, house cleaning *Bad for: most activities*	*Rabbit*
Sat **18**	**Good for:** worship, prayer *Bad for: most activities*	*Dragon*
Sun **19**	**Good for:** school, worship *Bad for: wedding, grand opening, travel*	*Snake*
Mon **20**	**Good for:** most activities *Bad for: funeral, lawsuit*	*Horse*
Tue **21**	⬛ **DON'T DO IMPORTANT THINGS** ⬛	*Sheep*
Wed **22**	**Good for:** grand opening, wedding, contract *Bad for: hunting, surgery*	*Monkey*
Thu **23**	**Good for:** wedding, grand opening, business *Bad for: burial, funeral*	*Rooster*
Fri **24**	**Good for:** worship, prayer *Bad for: most activities*	*Dog*
Sat **25**	**Good for:** begin mission, school, planting *Bad for: funeral, lawsuit*	*Pig*
Sun **26**	⬛ **DON'T DO IMPORTANT THINGS** ⬛	*Rat*
Mon **27**	**Good for:** contract, business, buy property *Bad for: moving, travel, fix house*	*Ox*
Tue **28**	**Good for:** prayer, house cleaning *Bad for: wedding, grand opening*	*Tiger*
Wed **29**	**Good for:** prayer, house cleaning *Bad for: most activities*	*Rabbit*
Thu **30**	**Good for:** worship, prayer *Bad for: most activities*	*Dragon*
Fri **31**	**Good for:** business, begin mission, ground digging *Bad for: lawsuit*	*Snake*

S	M	T	W	T	F	S
						1
2	3	4	5	6	7	8
9	10	11	12	13	14	15
16	17	18	19	20	21	22
23	24	25	26	27	28	29
30	31					

August 2020

unfavorable for:

Sat **1**	**Good for:** house cleaning, prayer *Bad for: most activities*	*Horse*
Sun **2**	⊖ **DON'T DO IMPORTANT THINGS** ⊖	*Sheep*
Mon **3**	**Good for:** contract, construction, buy property *Bad for: funeral, lawsuit*	*Monkey*
Tue **4**	**Good for:** most activities *Bad for: burial, funeral*	*Rooster*
Wed **5**	**Good for:** worship, prayer *Bad for: most activities*	*Dog*
Thu **6**	**Good for:** begin mission, school, planting *Bad for: funeral, lawsuit*	*Pig*
Fri **7**	⊖ **DON'T DO IMPORTANT THINGS** ⊖	*Rat*
Sat **8**	**Good for:** worship, prayer *Bad for: most activities*	*Ox*
Sun **9**	**Good for:** wedding, school, prayer *Bad for: contract, buy property*	*Tiger*
Mon **10**	**Good for:** burial, ground digging *Bad for: wedding, grand opening, begin mission*	*Rabbit*
Tue **11**	**Good for:** planting, worship *Bad for: contract, business*	*Dragon*
Wed **12**	**Good for:** wedding, grand opening, business *Bad for: burial, ground digging*	*Snake*
Thu **13**	**Good for:** most activities *Bad for: funeral, lawsuit*	*Horse*
Fri **14**	**Good for:** prayer, planting *Bad for: lawsuit, contract*	*Sheep*
Sat **15**	⊖ **DON'T DO IMPORTANT THINGS** ⊖	*Monkey*

Sun **16**	**Good for:** worship, prayer *Bad for: most activities*	*Rooster*
Mon **17**	**Good for:** contract, business, buy property *Bad for: moving, travel, fix house*	*Dog*
Tue **18**	**Good for:** most activities *Bad for: hunting, surgery*	*Pig*
Wed **19**	⊖ **DON'T DO IMPORTANT THINGS** ⊖	*Rat*
Thu **20**	**Good for:** school, worship *Bad for: wedding, grand opening, travel*	*Ox*
Fri **21**	**Good for:** worship, prayer *Bad for: wedding, grand opening, begin mission*	*Tiger*
Sat **22**	**Good for:** contract, business, buy property *Bad for: funeral, lawsuit*	*Rabbit*
Sun **23**	**Good for:** most activities *Bad for: hunting, surgery*	*Dragon*
Mon **24**	⊖ **DON'T DO IMPORTANT THINGS** ⊖	*Snake*
Tue **25**	**Good for:** wedding, construction, buy property *Bad for: funeral, lawsuit*	*Horse*
Wed **26**	**Good for:** house cleaning, prayer *Bad for: most activities*	*Sheep*
Thu **27**	⊖ **DON'T DO IMPORTANT THINGS** ⊖	*Monkey*
Fri **28**	**Good for:** wedding, grand opening, business *Bad for: burial, ground digging*	*Rooster*
Sat **29**	**Good for:** worship, prayer *Bad for: most activities*	*Dog*
Sun **30**	**Good for:** school, worship *Bad for: wedding, grand opening, begin mission*	*Pig*
Mon **31**	⊖ **DON'T DO IMPORTANT THINGS** ⊖	*Rat*

S	M	T	W	T	F	S
		1	2	3	4	5
6	7	8	9	10	11	12
13	14	15	16	17	18	19
20	21	22	23	24	25	26
27	28	29	30			

September 2020

unfavorable for:

Tue 1	**Good for:** worship, prayer **Bad for:** contract, business	Ox
Wed 2	**Good for:** most activities **Bad for:** funeral, lawsuit	Tiger
Thu 3	**Good for:** burial, ground digging **Bad for:** most activities	Rabbit
Fri 4	**Good for:** player, planting **Bad for:** lawsuit, contract	Dragon
Sat 5	**Good for:** worship, prayer **Bad for:** wedding, grand opening, contract	Snake
Sun 6	**Good for:** most activities **Bad for:** hunting, surgery	Horse
Mon 7	**Good for:** begin mission, ground digging , prayer **Bad for:** wedding, lawsuit	Sheep
Tue 8	**Good for:** worship, prayer **Bad for:** most activities	Monkey
Wed 9	⊖ **DON'T DO IMPORTANT THINGS** ⊖	Rooster
Thu 10	**Good for:** school, worship **Bad for:** wedding, grand opening, travel	Dog
Fri 11	**Good for:** most activities **Bad for:** burial, funeral	Pig
Sat 12	**Good for:** planting, worship **Bad for:** contract, business	Rat
Sun 13	**Good for:** wedding, grand opening, business **Bad for:** burial, ground digging	Ox
Mon 14	**Good for:** burial, ground digging **Bad for:** grand opening, contract	Tiger
Tue 15	**Good for:** planting, fix house **Bad for:** grand opening, begin mission	Rabbit

Wed **16**	**Good for:** begin mission, contract, planting *Bad for: lawsuit, surgery*	*Dragon*
Thu **17**	**Good for:** worship, prayer *Bad for: most activities*	*Snake*
Fri **18**	**Good for:** house cleaning *Bad for: most activities*	*Horse*
Sat **19**	**Good for:** wedding, grand opening *Bad for: burial, funeral*	*Sheep*
Sun **20**	**Good for:** prayer, house cleaning *Bad for: wedding, grand opening*	*Monkey*
Mon **21**	⚫ **DON'T DO IMPORTANT THINGS** ⚫	*Rooster*
Tue **22**	**Good for:** worship, prayer *Bad for: most activities*	*Dog*
Wed **23**	**Good for:** most activities *Bad for: surgery, hunting*	*Pig*
Thu **24**	⚫ **DON'T DO IMPORTANT THINGS** ⚫	*Rat*
Fri **25**	**Good for:** wedding, grand opening, business *Bad for: burial, ground digging*	*Ox*
Sat **26**	**Good for:** house cleaning, worship, prayer *Bad for: most activities*	*Tiger*
Sun **27**	**Good for:** business, worship, prayer *Bad for: most activities*	*Rabbit*
Mon **28**	**Good for:** begin mission, school, planting *Bad for: funeral, lawsuit*	*Dragon*
Tue **29**	**Good for:** wedding, grand opening, business *Bad for: funeral, lawsuit*	*Snake*
Wed **30**	**Good for:** worship, prayer *Bad for: wedding, grand opening, business*	*Horse*

S	M	T	W	T	F	S
				1	2	3
4	5	6	7	8	9	10
11	12	13	14	15	16	17
18	19	20	21	22	23	24
25	26	27	28	29	30	31

October 2020

unfavorable for:

Day		Unfavorable
Thu 1	**Good for:** weddding, contract, grand opening *Bad for: burial, funeral*	*Sheep*
Fri 2	**Good for:** worship, prayer *Bad for: most activities*	*Monkey*
Sat 3	⊖ **DON'T DO IMPORTANT THINGS** ⊖	*Rooster*
Sun 4	**Good for:** wedding, grand opening, business *Bad for: funeral, lawsuit*	*Dog*
Mon 5	**Good for:** most activities *Bad for: hunting, surgery*	*Pig*
Tue 6	⊖ **DON'T DO IMPORTANT THINGS** ⊖	*Rat*
Wed 7	**Good for:** wedding, contract, grand opening *Bad for: burial, ground digging*	*Ox*
Thu 8	**Good for:** contract, construction, buy property *Bad for: funeral, lawsuit*	*Tiger*
Fri 9	**Good for:** worship, prayer *Bad for: most activities*	*Rabbit*
Sat 10	**Good for:** wedding, grand opening, business *Bad for: burial, ground digging*	*Dragon*
Sun 11	**Good for:** prayer, house cleaning *Bad for: most activities*	*Snake*
Mon 12	**Good for:** worship, prayer *Bad for: contract, business, wedding, grand opening*	*Horse*
Tue 13	**Good for:** school, worship *Bad for: most activities*	*Sheep*
Wed 14	**Good for:** house cleaning *Bad for: wedding, grand opening*	*Monkey*
Thu 15	**Good for:** most activities *Bad for: funeral, lawsuit*	*Rooster*

Fri **16**	⊖ **DON'T DO IMPORTANT THINGS** ⊖	*Dog*
Sat **17**	**Good for:** wedding, grand opening, business *Bad for: burial, funeral*	*Pig*
Sun **18**	⊖ **DON'T DO IMPORTANT THINGS** ⊖	*Rat*
Mon **19**	**Good for:** worship, prayer *Bad for: most activities*	*Ox*
Tue **20**	**Good for:** grand opening, wedding, contract *Bad for: hunting, surgery*	*Tiger*
Wed **21**	**Good for:** worship *Bad for: wedding, grand opening, travel*	*Rabbit*
Thu **22**	**Good for:** house cleaning *Bad for: most activities*	*Dragon*
Fri **23**	**Good for:** worship, prayer *Bad for: most activities*	*Snake*
Sat **24**	**Good for:** worship, prayer *Bad for: wedding, grand opening, business*	*Horse*
Sun **25**	**Good for:** house cleaning *Bad for: begin mission, wedding, construction*	*Sheep*
Mon **26**	**Good for:** prayer, house cleaning *Bad for: moving, wedding, grand opening*	*Monkey*
Tue **27**	**Good for:** most activities *Bad for: funeral, lawsuit*	*Rooster*
Wed **28**	⊖ **DON'T DO IMPORTANT THINGS** ⊖	*Dog*
Thu **29**	**Good for:** begin mission, school, planting *Bad for: grand opening, wedding, contract*	*Pig*
Fri **30**	⊖ **DON'T DO IMPORTANT THINGS** ⊖	*Rat*
Sat **31**	**Good for:** worship, prayer *Bad for: most activities*	*Ox*

S	M	T	W	T	F	S
1	2	3	4	5	6	7
8	9	10	11	12	13	14
15	16	17	18	19	20	21
22	23	24	25	26	27	28
29	30					

November 2020

unfavorable for:

Day	Activities	Unfavorable
Sun **1**	**Good for:** wedding, grand opening, business **Bad for:** funeral, lawsuit	*Tiger*
Mon **2**	**Good for:** house cleaning **Bad for:** most activities	*Rabbit*
Tue **3**	**Good for:** moving, worship, prayer **Bad for:** wedding, grand opening, travel	*Dragon*
Wed **4**	**Good for:** contract, business, buy property **Bad for:** burial, ground digging	*Snake*
Thu **5**	**Good for:** prayer, house cleaning **Bad for:** begin mission, wedding, construction	*Horse*
Fri **6**	**Good for:** worship, prayer **Bad for:** most activities	*Sheep*
Sat **7**	**Good for:** contract, construction, buy property **Bad for:** funeral, lawsuit	*Monkey*
Sun **8**	**Good for:** most activities **Bad for:** hunting, surgery	*Rooster*
Mon **9**	**Good for:** house cleaning **Bad for:** most activities	*Dog*
Tue **10**	⊖ **DON'T DO IMPORTANT THINGS** ⊖	*Pig*
Wed **11**	⊖ **DON'T DO IMPORTANT THINGS** ⊖	*Rat*
Thu **12**	**Good for:** contract, business, buy property **Bad for:** moving, travel, fix house	*Ox*
Fri **13**	**Good for:** burial, ground digging **Bad for:** wedding, buy property, begin mission	*Tiger*
Sat **14**	**Good for:** school, worship **Bad for:** prayer, house cleaning	*Rabbit*
Sun **15**	**Good for:** worship, prayer **Bad for:** most activities	*Dragon*

Mon **16**	**Good for:** prayer, house cleaning ***Bad for:*** *wedding, grand opening, travel*	*Snake*
Tue **17**	**Good for:** most activities ***Bad for:*** *burial, funeral*	*Horse*
Wed **18**	**Good for:** worship, prayer ***Bad for:*** *most activities*	*Sheep*
Thu **19**	**Good for:** most activities ***Bad for:*** *funeral, lawsuit*	*Monkey*
Fri **20**	**Good for:** wedding, grand opening, business ***Bad for:*** *burial, funeral*	*Rooster*
Sat **21**	**Good for:** house cleaning ***Bad for:*** *most activities*	*Dog*
Sun **22**	⊖ **DON'T DO IMPORTANT THINGS** ⊖	*Pig*
Mon **23**	⊖ **DON'T DO IMPORTANT THINGS** ⊖	*Rat*
Tue **24**	**Good for:** contract, business, buy property ***Bad for:*** *moving, travel, fix house*	*Ox*
Wed **25**	**Good for:** worship, prayer ***Bad for:*** *most activities*	*Tiger*
Thu **26**	**Good for:** school , worship ***Bad for:*** *wedding, grand opening, travel*	*Rabbit*
Fri **27**	**Good for:** prayer, planting ***Bad for:*** *most activities*	*Dragon*
Sat **28**	**Good for:** worship, prayer, planting ***Bad for:*** *most activities*	*Snake*
Sun **29**	**Good for:** burial, ground digging, school ***Bad for:*** *wedding, grand opening, travel*	*Horse*
Mon **30**	**Good for:** worship, prayer ***Bad for:*** *begin mission, wedding, construction*	*Sheep*

S	M	T	W	T	F	S
		1	2	3	4	5
6	7	8	9	10	11	12
13	14	15	16	17	18	19
20	21	22	23	24	25	26
27	28	29	30	31		

December 2020

unfavorable for:

Tue **1**	**Good for:** wedding, buy property, begin mission *Bad for: ground digging*	*Monkey*
Wed **2**	**Good for:** most activities *Bad for: burial, funeral*	*Rooster*
Thu **3**	**Good for:** begin mission, wedding, construction *Bad for: burial, ground digging*	*Dog*
Fri **4**	⚊ **DON'T DO IMPORTANT THINGS** ⚊	*Pig*
Sat **5**	⚊ **DON'T DO IMPORTANT THINGS** ⚊	*Rat*
Sun **6**	**Good for:** contract, construction, buy property *Bad for: funeral, lawsuit*	*Ox*
Mon **7**	**Good for:** wedding, grand opening, business *Bad for: burial, ground digging*	*Tiger*
Tue **8**	**Good for:** worship, prayer *Bad for: most activities*	*Rabbit*
Wed **9**	**Good for:** prayer, planting *Bad for: lawsuit, contract*	*Dragon*
Thu **10**	**Good for:** planting, worship *Bad for: most activities*	*Snake*
Fri **11**	**Good for:** house cleaning *Bad for: begin mission, wedding, construction*	*Horse*
Sat **12**	**Good for:** prayer, house cleaning *Bad for: begin mission, wedding, construction*	*Sheep*
Sun **13**	**Good for:** wedding, grand opening, business *Bad for: burial, funeral*	*Monkey*
Mon **14**	**Good for:** worship, prayer *Bad for: most activities*	*Rooster*
Tue **15**	**Good for:** most activities *Bad for: funeral, lawsuit*	*Dog*

Wed **16**	**Good for:** burial, ground digging, worship, prayer *Bad for: most activities*	*Pig*
Thu **17**	⊖ **DON'T DO IMPORTANT THINGS** ⊖	*Rat*
Fri **18**	**Good for:** worship, prayer *Bad for: wedding, contract, grand opening*	*Ox*
Sat **19**	**Good for:** worship, prayer *Bad for: contract, business*	*Tiger*
Sun **20**	**Good for:** prayer, house cleaning *Bad for: most activities*	*Rabbit*
Mon **21**	**Good for:** worship, prayer *Bad for: grand opening, begin mission*	*Dragon*
Tue **22**	**Good for:** school, worship *Bad for: wedding, grand opening, travel*	*Snake*
Wed **23**	**Good for:** worship, prayer *Bad for: most activities*	*Horse*
Thu **24**	**Good for:** most activities *Bad for: hunting, surgery*	*Sheep*
Fri **25**	**Good for:** wedding, grand opening, business *Bad for: burial, funeral*	*Monkey*
Sat **26**	**Good for:** house cleaning *Bad for: most activities*	*Rooster*
Sun **27**	**Good for:** wedding, grand opening, business *Bad for: funeral, lawsuit*	*Dog*
Mon **28**	**Good for:** burial, ground digging, worship, prayer *Bad for: wedding, contract, grand opening*	*Pig*
Tue **29**	⊖ **DON'T DO IMPORTANT THINGS** ⊖	*Rat*
Wed **30**	**Good for:** worship, prayer *Bad for: most activities*	*Ox*
Thu **31**	**Good for:** contract, business, buy property *Bad for: ground digging, surgery*	*Tiger*

January 2021

unfavorable for:

Day	Activities	Unfavorable
Fri 1	**Good for:** prayer, house cleaning **Bad for:** wedding, grand opening	*Rabbit*
Sat 2	**Good for:** begin mission, school, planting **Bad for:** *funeral, lawsuit*	*Dragon*
Sun 3	**Good for:** school, worship **Bad for:** *most activities*	*Snake*
Mon 4	**Good for:** house cleaning **Bad for:** *begin mission, wedding, construction*	*Horse*
Tue 5	**Good for:** worship, prayer **Bad for:** *most activities*	*Sheep*
Wed 6	**Good for:** house cleaning **Bad for:** *wedding, grand opening, travel*	*Monkey*
Thu 7	**Good for:** most activities **Bad for:** *burial, ground digging*	*Rooster*
Fri 8	**Good for:** prayer, house cleaning **Bad for:** *most activities*	*Dog*
Sat 9	**Good for:** worship, prayer **Bad for:** *begin mission, wedding, construction*	*Pig*
Sun 10	⊖ **DON'T DO IMPORTANT THINGS** ⊖	*Rat*
Mon 11	⊖ **DON'T DO IMPORTANT THINGS** ⊖	*Ox*
Tue 12	**Good for:** contract, construction, buy property **Bad for:** *funeral, lawsuit*	*Tiger*
Wed 13	**Good for:** most activities **Bad for:** *funeral, lawsuit*	*Rabbit*
Thu 14	**Good for:** school, worship **Bad for:** *wedding, grand opening, travel*	*Dragon*
Fri 15	**Good for:** worship, prayer **Bad for:** *most activities*	*Snake*

Sat **16**	**Good for:** worship, burial, ground digging *Bad for: lawsuit, surgery*	*Horse*
Sun **17**	**Good for:** contract, business, buy property *Bad for: burial, ground digging*	*Sheep*
Mon **18**	**Good for:** prayer, house cleaning *Bad for: wedding, grand opening, travel*	*Monkey*
Tue **19**	**Good for:** planting, worship *Bad for: contract, business*	*Rooster*
Wed **20**	**Good for:** school, worship *Bad for: begin mission, wedding, construction*	*Dog*
Thu **21**	**Good for:** most activities *Bad for: burial, funeral*	*Pig*
Fri **22**	**Good for:** grand opening, wedding, contract *Bad for: hunting, surgery*	*Rat*
Sat **23**	⊖ **DON'T DO IMPORTANT THINGS** ⊖	*Ox*
Sun **24**	**Good for:** worship, prayer *Bad for: most activities*	*Tiger*
Mon **25**	**Good for:** wedding, business, buy property *Bad for: ground digging, surgery*	*Rabbit*
Tue **26**	**Good for:** worship, prayer *Bad for: contract, business*	*Dragon*
Wed **27**	**Good for:** contract, business, buy property *Bad for: moving, travel, fix house*	*Snake*
Thu **28**	**Good for:** burial, worship, prayer *Bad for: moving, ground digging*	*Horse*
Fri **29**	**Good for:** worship, prayer *Bad for: most activities*	*Sheep*
Sat **30**	**Good for:** school, worship *Bad for: begin mission, wedding, construction*	*Monkey*
Sun **31**	**Good for:** prayer, house cleaning *Bad for: wedding, grand opening*	*Rooster*

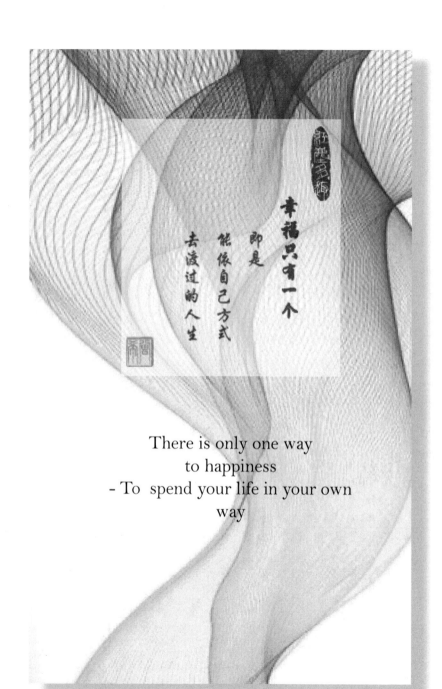

幸福只有一个
即是
能依自己方式
去渡过的人生

There is only one way
to happiness
- To spend your life in your own
way

TEN THOUSAND YEAR CALENDAR

TEN-THOUSAND YEAR CALENDAR

	1ST MONTH Wu Yin	2ND MONTH Ji Mao	3RD MONTH Geng Chen	4TH MONTH Xin Si	LEAP MONTH	5TH MONTH Ren Wu	6TH MONTH Gui Wei	
1	1/25 Ding Mao	2/23 Bing Shen	3/24 Bing Yin	4/23 Bing Shen	5/23 Bing Yin	6/21 Yi Wei	7/21 Yi Chou	1
2	1/26 Wu Chen	2/24 Ding You	3/25 Ding Mao	4/24 Ding You	5/24 Ding Mao	6/22 Bing Shen	7/22 Bing Yin	2
3	1/27 Ji Si	2/25 Wu Xu	3/26 Wu Chen	4/25 Wu Xu	5/25 Wu Chen	6/23 Ding You	7/23 Ding Mao	3
4	1/28 Geng Wu	2/26 Ji Hai	3/27 Ji Si	4/26 Ji Hai	5/26 Ji Si	6/24 Wu Xu	7/24 Wu Chen	4
5	1/29 Xin Wei	2/27 Geng Zi	3/28 Geng Wu	4/27 Geng Zi	5/27 Geng Wu	6/25 Ji Hai	7/25 Ji Si	5
6	1/30 Ren Shen	2/28 Xin Chou	3/29 Xin Wei	4/28 Xin Chou	5/28 Xin Wei	6/26 Geng Zi	7/26 Geng Wu	6
7	1/31 Gui You	2/29 Ren Yin	3/30 Ren Shen	4/29 Ren Yin	5/29 Ren Shen	6/27 Xin Chou	7/27 Xin Wei	7
8	2/1 Jia Xu	3/1 Gui Mao	3/31 Gui You	4/30 Gui Mao	5/30 Gui You	6/28 Ren Yin	7/28 Ren Shen	8
9	2/2 Yi Hai	3/2 Jia Chen	4/1 Jia Xu	5/1 Jia Chen	5/31 Jia Xu	6/29 Gui Mao	7/29 Gui You	9
10	2/3 Bing Zi	3/3 Yi Si	4/2 Yi Hai	5/2 Yi Si	6/1 Yi Hai	6/30 Jia Chen	7/30 Jia Xu	10
11	2/4 Ding Chou	3/4 Bing Wu	4/3 Bing Zi	5/3 Bing Wu	6/2 Bing Zi	7/1 Yi Si	7/31 Yi Hai	11
12	2/5 Wu Yin	3/5 Ding Wei	4/4 Ding Chou	5/4 Ding Wei	6/3 Ding Chou	7/2 Bing Wu	8/1 Bing Zi	12
13	2/6 Ji Mao	3/6 Wu Shen	4/5 Wu Yin	5/5 Wu Shen	6/4 Wu Yin	7/3 Ding Wei	8/2 Ding Chou	13
14	2/7 Geng Chen	3/7 Ji You	4/6 Ji Mao	5/6 Ji You	6/5 Ji Mao	7/4 Wu Shen	8/3 Wu Yin	14
15	2/8 Xin Si	3/8 Geng Xu	4/7 Geng Chen	5/7 Geng Xu	6/6 Geng Chen	7/5 Ji You	8/4 Ji Mao	15
16	2/9 Ren Wu	3/9 Xin Hai	4/8 Xin Si	5/8 Xin Hai	6/7 Xin Si	7/6 Geng Xu	8/5 Geng Chen	16
17	2/10 Gui Wei	3/10 Ren Zi	4/9 Ren Wu	5/9 Ren Zi	6/8 Ren Wu	7/7 Xin Hai	8/6 Xin Si	17
18	2/11 Jia Shen	3/11 Gui Chou	4/10 Gui Wei	5/10 Gui Chou	6/9 Gui Wei	7/8 Ren Zi	8/7 Ren Wu	18
19	2/12 Yi You	3/12 Jia Yin	4/11 Jia Shen	5/11 Jia Yin	6/10 Jia Shen	7/9 Gui Chou	8/8 Gui Wei	19
20	2/13 Bing Xu	3/13 Yi Mao	4/12 Yi You	5/12 Yi Mao	6/11 Yi You	7/10 Jia Yin	8/9 Jia Shen	20
21	2/14 Ding Hai	3/14 Bing Chen	4/13 Bing Xu	5/13 Bing Chen	6/12 Bing Xu	7/11 Yi Mao	8/10 Yi You	21
22	2/15 Wu Zi	3/15 Ding Si	4/14 Ding Hai	5/14 Ding Si	6/13 Ding Hai	7/12 Bing Chen	8/11 Bing Xu	22
23	2/16 Ji Chou	3/16 Wu Wu	4/15 Wu Zi	5/15 Wu Wu	6/14 Wu Zi	7/13 Ding Si	8/12 Ding Hai	23
24	2/17 Geng Yin	3/17 Ji Wei	4/16 Ji Chou	5/16 Ji Wei	6/15 Ji Chou	7/14 Wu Wu	8/13 Wu Zi	24
25	2/18 Xin Mao	3/18 Geng Shen	4/17 Geng Yin	5/17 Geng Shen	6/16 Geng Yin	7/15 Ji Wei	8/14 Ji Chou	25
26	2/19 Ren Chen	3/19 Xin You	4/18 Xin Mao	5/18 Xin You	6/17 Xin Mao	7/16 Geng Shen	8/15 Geng Yin	26
27	2/20 Gui Si	3/20 Ren Xu	4/19 Ren Chen	5/19 Ren Xu	6/18 Ren Chen	7/17 Xin You	8/16 Xin Mao	27
28	2/21 Jia Wu	3/21 Gui Hai	4/20 Gui Si	5/20 Gui Hai	6/19 Gui Si	7/18 Ren Xu	8/17 Ren Chen	28
29	2/22 Yi Wei	3/22 Jia Zi	4/21 Jia Wu	5/21 Jia Zi	6/20 Jia Wu	7/19 Gui Hai	8/18 Gui Si	29
30		3/23 Yi Chou	4/22 Yi Wei	5/22 Yi Chou		7/20 Jia Zi		30
	8 White	7 Red	6 White	5 Yellow		4 Green	3 Jade	
Jie	Li Chun 2/4 5:18pm	Jing Zhi 3/5 11:03am	Qing Ming 4/4 3:48pm	Li Xia 5/5 9:08am		Mang Zhong 6/5 1:22pm	Xiao Shu 7/6 11:46pm	Jie
Qi	Yu Shui 2/19 1:02pm	Chun Fen 3/20 11:53am	Gu Yu 4/19 10:55pm	Xiao Man 5/20 8:07pm		Xia Zhi 6/21 6:10am	Da Shu 7/22 5:16pm	Qi

Year: Geng Zi • 7 Red  2020

	7TH MONTH Jia Shen	8TH MONTH Yi You	9TH MONTH Bing Xu	10TH MONTH Ding Hai	11TH MONTH Wu Zi	12TH MONTH Ji Chou	
					2020-2021		
1	8/19 Jia Wu	9/17 Gui Hai	10/17 Gui Si	11/15 Ren Xu	12/15 Ren Chen	1/13 Xin You	1
2	8/20 Yi Wei	9/18 Jia Zi	10/18 Jia Wu	11/16 Gui Hai	12/16 Gui Si	1/14 Ren Xu	2
3	8/21 Bing Shen	9/19 Yi Chou	10/19 Yi Wei	11/17 Jia Zi	12/17 Jia Wu	1/15 Gui Hai	3
4	8/22 Ding You	9/20 Bing Yin	10/20 Bing Shen	11/18 Yi Chou	12/18 Yi Wei	1/16 Jia Zi	4
5	8/23 Wu Xu	9/21 Ding Mao	10/21 Ding You	11/19 Bing Yin	12/19 Bing Shen	1/17 Yi Chou	5
6	8/24 Ji Hai	9/22 Wu Chen	10/22 Wu Xu	11/20 Ding Mao	12/20 Ding You	1/18 Bing Yin	6
7	8/25 Geng Zi	9/23 Ji Si	10/23 Ji Hai	11/21 Wu Chen	12/21 Wu Xu	1/19 Ding Mao	7
8	8/26 Xin Chou	9/24 Geng Wu	10/24 Geng Zi	11/22 Ji Si	12/22 Ji Hai	1/20 Wu Chen	8
9	8/27 Ren Yin	9/25 Xin Wei	10/25 Xin Chou	11/23 Geng Wu	12/23 Geng Zi	1/21 Ji Si	9
10	8/28 Gui Mao	9/26 Ren Shen	10/26 Ren Yin	11/24 Xin Wei	12/24 Xin Chou	1/22 Geng Wu	10
11	8/29 Jia Chen	9/27 Gui You	10/27 Gui Mao	11/25 Ren Shen	12/25 Ren Yin	1/23 Xin Wei	11
12	8/30 Yi Si	9/28 Jia Xu	10/28 Jia Chen	11/26 Gui You	12/26 Gui Mao	1/24 Ren Shen	12
13	8/31 Bing Wu	9/29 Yi Hai	10/29 Yi Si	11/27 Jia Xu	12/27 Jia Chen	1/25 Gui You	13
14	9/1 Ding Wei	9/30 Bing Zi	10/30 Bing Wu	11/28 Yi Hai	12/28 Yi Si	1/26 Jia Xu	14
15	9/2 Wu Shen	10/1 Ding Chou	10/31 Ding Wei	11/29 Bing Zi	12/29 Bing Wu	1/27 Yi Hai	15
16	9/3 Ji You	10/2 Wu Yin	11/1 Wu Shen	11/30 Ding Chou	12/30 Ding Wei	1/28 Bing Zi	16
17	9/4 Geng Xu	10/3 Ji Mao	11/2 Ji You	12/1 Wu Yin	12/31 Wu Shen	1/29 Ding Chou	17
18	9/5 Xin Hai	10/4 Geng Chen	11/3 Geng Xu	12/2 Ji Mao	1/1 Ji You	1/30 Wu Yin	18
19	9/6 Ren Zi	10/5 Xin Si	11/4 Xin Hai	12/3 Geng Chen	1/2 Geng Xu	1/31 Ji Mao	19
20	9/7 Gui Chou	10/6 Ren Wu	11/5 Ren Zi	12/4 Xin Si	1/3 Xin Hai	2/1 Geng Chen	20
21	9/8 Jia Yin	10/7 Gui Wei	11/6 Gui Chou	12/5 Ren Wu	1/4 Ren Zi	2/2 Xin Si	21
22	9/9 Yi Mao	10/8 Jia Shen	11/7 Jia Yin	12/6 Gui Wei	1/5 Gui Chou	2/3 Ren Wu	22
23	9/10 Bing Chen	10/9 Yi You	11/8 Yi Mao	12/7 Jia Shen	1/6 Jia Yin	2/4 Gui Wei	23
24	9/11 Ding Si	10/10 Bing Xu	11/9 Bing Chen	12/8 Yi You	1/7 Yi Mao	2/5 Jia Shen	24
25	9/12 Wu Wu	10/11 Ding Hai	11/10 Ding Si	12/9 Bing Xu	1/8 Bing Chen	2/6 Yi You	25
26	9/13 Ji Wei	10/12 Wu Zi	11/11 Wu Wu	12/10 Ding Hai	1/9 Ding Si	2/7 Bing Xu	26
27	9/14 Geng Shen	10/13 Ji Chou	11/12 Ji Wei	12/11 Wu Zi	1/10 Wu Wu	2/8 Ding Hai	27
28	9/15 Xin You	10/14 Geng Yin	11/13 Geng Shen	12/12 Ji Chou	1/11 Ji Wei	2/9 Wu Zi	28
29	9/16 Ren Xu	10/15 Xin Mao	11/14 Xin You	12/13 Geng Yin	1/12 Geng Shen	2/10 Ji Chou	29
30		10/16 Ren Chen		12/14 Xin Mao		2/11 Geng Yin	30
	2 Black	1 White	9 Purple	8 White	7 Red	6 White	
Jie	Li Qiu 8/7 9:51am	Bai Lu 9/7 1:12pm	Han Lu 10/8 5:15am	Li Dong 11/7 8:31am	Da Xue 12/7 1:09am	Xiao Han 1/5 11:55am	Jie
Qi	Chu Shu 8/23 12:43am	Qiu Fen 9/23 8:49pm	Shuang Jiang 10/23 8:26am	Xiao Xue 11/22 5:56am	Dong Zhi 12/21 6:54pm	Da Han 1/20 5:04am	Qi

The Principles of Feng Shui - Book One

After years of intensive research, experimentation, exploration and teaching of Feng Shui, Master Larry Sang put forth his accumulated knowledge and insights into this book. This book will systematically introduce Feng Shui to its readers. This book is recommended for our Beginning, Intermediate and Advanced Feng Shui classes.

Available in paperback and ebook. $18.75 US

Yi Jing for Love and Marriage

In the journey of life, we often experience times of doubt, confusion and feeling lost. What should we do when facing this type of situation? The Changing Hexagram Divination method can help by predicting what may happen. It can provide guidelines for coping with difficult situations or insight into beneficial ones. This book provides a simple method for the reader to predict the answers to their questions and to help others. Besides resolving confusion and doubt, it also provides a fun hobby for those interested in the ancient art of divination. Use this book as your consultant on Love and Marriage when the need arises!

Available in paperback and ebook. $14.75 US

Ten-Thousand Year Calendar (1882 - 2031)

Normally printed in Chinese, but now in English, this handy reference guide is what the Chinese call the Ten-Thousand Year Calendar. This calendar contains information for 150 years, from 1882 to 2031. It gives the annual, monthly, and daily stem and branch, the annual and monthly flying Star, as well as the lunar day of the month. It also gives information about the lunar and solar months, the solstices, equinoxes, and the beginning of the four seasons in the Chinese calendar. The Ten-Thousand Year Calendar is used for Feng Shui, Chinese Astrology, Day Selection, and various predictive techniques.

Available in ebook only. $26.00 US

Feng Shui Facts and Myths

This book is a collection of stories about Feng Shui and Astrology. Master Sang attempts to explain aspects of Feng Shui and Chinese Astrology, as the terms are understood or misunderstood in the West. This book will provide you with deeper information on the Chinese culture traditions of Feng Shui and Astrology.

Available in paperback and ebook. $16.00 US

Larry Sang's
2020 Chinese Astrology & Feng Shui Guide
The Year of The Rat

Each Section explains how to determine the key piece: determining your animal sign; how to read the Feng Shui of your home; and how to read the Day Selection calendar - a valuable day by day indication of favorable and unfavorable activity.

Available in paperback and ebook. $16.50 US

COURSE CATALOG

The following is a current list of the courses available from *The American Feng Shui Institute.* Please consult our online catalog for course fees, descriptions and new additions.

FENG SHUI

CLASS	CLASS NAME	PREREQUISITE
FS095	Introduction to Feng Shui	
FS101/OL	Beginning Feng Shui & Online	-
FS102/OL	Intermediate Feng Shui & Online	-
FS201/OL	Advanced Feng Shui & Online	FS101+FS102/OL
FS205/OL	Advanced Sitting and Facing & Online	FS101+FS102/OL
FS106/OL	Additional Concepts on Sitting & Facing	FS102/OL
FS225	Feng Shui Folk Beliefs	FS201
FS227/OL	Professional Skills for Feng Shui Consultants	FS201
FS231	Feng Shui Yourself & Your Business	FS201
FS235	Symptoms of a House	FS201
FS250	Explanation of Advanced Feng Shui Theories	FS201
FS275	9 Palace Grid and Pie Chart Graph Usage & Online	FS201
FS280	Advanced East West Theory	FS201
FS301	Advanced Feng Shui Case Study 1 & 2	FS201
FS303	Advanced Feng Shui Case Study 3 & 4 + Online	FS201
FS305/OL	Advanced Feng Shui Case Study 5 & Online	FS201
FS306/OL	Advanced Feng Shui Case Study 6 & Online	FS201
FS307/OL	Advanced Feng Shui Case Study 7 & Online	FS201
FS308/OL	Advanced Feng Shui Case Study 8 & Online	FS201
FS309	Advanced Feng Shui Case Study 9 & 10	FS201
FS311	Advanced Feng Shui Case Study 11	FS201
FS312/OL	Advanced Feng Shui Case Study 12	FS201
FS313/OL	Advanced Feng Shui Case Study 13 & Online	FS201 & AS101
FS314	Advanced Feng Shui Case Study 14	FS201
FS315	Advanced Feng Shui Case Study 15	FS201
FS316/FS317	Advanced Feng Shui Case Study 16 & 17	FS201
FS318/FS319	Advanced Feng Shui Case Study 18 & 19	FS201
FS320/FS321	Advanced Feng Shui Case Study 20 & 21	FS201
FS322/FS323	Advanced Feng Shui Case Study 22 & 23	FS201 & AS101
FS324/FS325	Advanced Feng Shui Case Study 24 & 25	FS201
FS326/FS327	Advanced Feng Shui Case Study 26 & 27	FS201

FENG SHUI - *continued from previous page*

FS340/OL	Secrets of the Five Ghosts	FS201
FS341	The Secrets of the "San Ban Gua"	FS201
FS260/OL	Lawsuit Support & Online	FS201 & AS101
FS270/OL	The Taisui, Year Breaker, Three Sha & Online	FS201 & AS101
FS350/OL	Feng Shui Day Selection 1 & Online	FS201 & AS101
FS351/OL	Feng Shui Day Selection 2 & Online	FS201 & FS350/OL
FS360/OL	Marriage and Life Partner Selection Online	FS201 & AS101
FS375/OL	Introduction to Yin House Feng Shui	FS201

YI JING

YJ101	Beginning Yi Jing Divination	AS101
YJ102	Yi Jing Coin Divination	AS101
YJ103	Plum Flower Yi Jing Calculation	AS101

CHINESE ASTROLOGY

AS101	Stems and Branches & Online	-
AS102	Four Pillars 1 & 2 (Zi Ping Ba Zi)	AS101 or AS101/OL
AS103	Four Pillars 3 & 4 (Zi Ping Ba Zi)	AS102
AS105	Four Pillars 5 & 6 (Zi Ping Ba Zi)	AS103
AS201A/OL	Beginning Zi Wei Dou Shu, Part 1	AS101
AS201B/OL	Beginning Zi Wei Dou Shu, Part 2	AS201A/OL
AS211/OL	Intermediate Zi Wei Dou Shu	AS201B/OL
AS301A/OL	Advanced Zi Wei Dou Shu, Part 1	AS211/OL
AS301B/OL	Advanced Zi Wei Dou Shu, Part 2	AS201A/OL
AS311/OL	Zi Wei Dou Shu Case Study 1 & Online	AS301B/OL
AS313/OL	Zi Wei Dou Shu Case Study 3 & Online	AS301B/OL
AS314	Zi Wei Dou Shu Case Study 2 & 4	AS301B/OL

CHINESE ARTS

CA101/OL	Palm & Face Reading 1 & 2	-
CA102	Palm & Face Reading 3 & 4	CA101 or CA101/OL
CA103	Palm & Face Reading for Health	-
CA121	Introduction to Chinese Medicine	-
CA110	Professional Face Reading	-

CHINESE PHILOSOPHY

CP101	Introduction to Daode Jing	-
CP102	Feng Shui Yourself	-

CLASSES AT THE
AMERICAN FENG SHUI INSTITUTE

Due to the limited seating capacity, reservations are necessary and seats are on a first come first serve basis. To reserve your seat, a $50.00 US deposit is required and is non-refundable if cancellation by student takes place less than three days before class. Please mail-in check or call us to reserve your seat with a credit card*. Balance is due on the first day of class.

Please DO NOT e-mail credit card information as this is not a secure method

ONLINE CLASSES WITH THE
AMERICAN FENG SHUI INSTITUTE FEATURE:

- Easy navigation
- Self tests at the end of each module
- A discussion board with trained Institute's Instructors
- Audio clips for pronunciation
- An online discussion board
- An instant feedback final exam

The online classes are self-paced study modules. They are segmented into four, one-week lessons that lead you at your own pace, over the four-week course. You have 60 days to complete the course work.

For more information, please see our website:
www.amfengshui.com

AMERICAN
FENG SHUI

INSTITUTE

7220 N. Rosemead Blvd.
Suite. 204
San Gabriel, CA 91775
Phone: (626) 571-2757

E-mail: fsinfo@amfengshui.com
amfengshui@gmail.com